FACTFINDER GUIDE

CATS

FACTFINDER GUIDE

CATS

Marianne Mays

This edition published in 1999 by
An imprint of Grange Books PLC
The Grange, Kingsnorth Industrial Estate
Hoo, nr. Rochester, Kent
ME3 9ND

Produced by PRC Publishing Ltd,
Kiln House, 210 New Kings Road, London SW6 4NZ

ISBN 1 84013 304 X

Printed and bound in China

CONTENTS

INTRODUCTION

The History of the Cat

The exact origins of the pet, or domestic, cat, are not entirely known. It is believed to have developed from various types of small wild cats — there are approximately 25 different species of smaller, wild cats worldwide (that is, cats that are smaller than lions, tigers, and the like) and many of these can interbreed with each other. Out of these 25, three species in particular are considered to be the most likely ancestors of the domestic cat: the African Wild Cat (*Felis libyca*), the Forest Wild Cat (*Felis silvestris*), or the Jungle Cat (*Felis chaus*).

The Forest Wild Cat is closely related to the African Wild Cat, and can be found in mainland Europe and Great Britain. The Jungle Cat was already domesticated by Ancient Egyptians as far back as 2000 BC. During the centuries, humans domesticated all of these species, and doubtless also interbred them with each other, resulting in a mixture which eventually became our domestic cat (*Felis cattus*).

The first civilized culture to domesticate cats were the Ancient Egyptians. It is likely that the first domestications were carried out for practical reasons — cats were used to catch and kill rats, mice, and other vermin; a practice which, of course, still continues today! As well as the smaller prey though, Egyptian tomb paintings, dating back to as early as 2000 BC, show cats that are apparently accompanying men in hunting expeditions, and being used in a manner similar to the way that the dog was used in hunting. These cats were undoubtedly domesticated Jungle Cats, and these may even have been trained to perform tasks such as retrieving game. There are however, no actual written records of such trained hunting cats and the only clue to their existence is to be found in these paintings. However, it cannot be proved if the paintings depicted actual occurrences, or if they were, perhaps, allegorical rather than factual.

Later, cats became revered as gods in Ancient Egypt, and were also sometimes considered to be reincarnations of priests. The most famous of these was Bast (also known as Bastet), the Egyptian goddess with the head of a cat on a woman's body. Bast was the goddess of fertility, and as such she attracted a large cult around her. A fertility goddess was, of course, immensely popular and in much demand and many festivals were held in her honor. Her popularity undoubtedly had a lot to do with the Egyptians love of cats. These animals became very pampered receiving all they could ever need, and being treated as household gods by the Ancient Egyptians. When a cat died, it often received the same treatment as a dead human being of importance — it was embalmed and mummified. Large numbers of cat mummies have been found during excavations, and these can be seen in various museums all over the world.

In 30 BC, Roman Legions conquered the Egypt of Cleopatra, and this led to the domesticated cat spreading to other parts of the world, as many cats were taken away from Egypt by Roman legionnaires. After this, the cat has never again been seen as a god, but it was then still considered to be lucky.

During the Middle Ages, humanity's view on the cat changed drastically — particularly in Europe. This coincided with the church's strong campaign against witchcraft, at which time cats became seen as agents of the devil and were persecuted in much the same way as women accused of being witches. Sometimes, such accusations would be leveled simply because a woman lived alone and kept a domestic cat. According to the church, cats were either agents of the devil or even a feline version of the devil himself. Accordingly, cats were caught, bundled into sacks, and burned on bonfires, similar to the way a witch would be burned and witnessed by large, cheering crowds. Cats could also be drowned, thrown to their death from tall buildings, or even hanged.

Once the witch-hunting frenzy started to die out, cats were left alone, and people started to realize that they were indeed very useful animals when kept as rat catchers. However, it was not until the 18th century that people began keeping cats simply as companions inside their own homes, and even then, this was mainly done by people of higher standing and affluence. Thus the cat gained an entirely new status; that of a pet.

After this, it did not take long before cats became kept as show animals. The very first cat show to be held anywhere in the world was staged by Harrison Weir, a well-known cat lover known as, "The Father of the Cat Fancy." Weir was an author and illustrator of cat books, as well as a dedicated breeder of pedigree cats. His first show was staged in 1871, in London at Crystal Palace. It was a deliberate attempt by Weir, to improve the status of the cat by presenting it as a show animal. The event was a success and led to many more being staged. Soon, a "Standard of Points" was drawn up, detailing how the ideal specimen of each breed should look. There appears to be some controversy regarding exactly when the first American cat show was staged — some sources stating that shows were held as early as the 1870s. The first "notable" cat show was held in 1881, at Bunnell's Museum in New York, and this event was reported in the *New York Times*. However, the first *official* American cat show was staged in 1895, at Madison Square Garden in New York City. This show was patterned after Harrison Weir's Crystal Palace show, and was deemed a great success. Exhibits included ocelots, wild cats, and civet cats, as well as ordinary domestic cats.

The cat had now truly arrived as a domestic pet alongside the dog, and in some countries, including the US and the UK, the cat is now more popular as a pet than its canine counterpart.

Types of Cat

Domestic cats can be broadly classified as being of different types, and the cats within one particular type group often show similar characteristics in looks and behavior. Thus, it makes very good sense to first decide what *type* of cat you would like to keep as a pet, before concentrating on deciding which particular breed to choose.

PERSIAN CATS
Probably the most popular breed of pedigree cat worldwide, the Persian comes in an abundance of different colors and markings. There is also a shorthaired version of the Persian, the Exotic Shorthair. Apart from the difference in coat length, the Persian and the Exotic are both very similar, and these are commonly both

classified as Longhair breeds — despite the fact that the Exotic is shorthaired. Persians and Exotics makes ideal pet cats, as they are generally very friendly, laid back, and placid cats that tolerate a lot of handling, even by children. Their appearance is also very appealing to most people; the body is short and cobby with thick, short legs, a very round face with a perfectly flat profile, large round eyes, and small ears. A Persian gives the impression of being the eternal kitten and its long fur also makes it a typical "chocolate box" cat. However, it must always be remembered that any Persian cat requires a great deal of grooming to keep the coat in good condition and free of knots and tangles. A neglected Persian coat is a very sorry sight, and it is cruel to allow a Persian to get into such a state that the only option left is to shave the coat off. For people who like the Persian looks and temperament, but feel somewhat daunted at the thought of all the necessary grooming, the Exotic Shorthair is an excellent alternative.

SHORTHAIR CATS
Including many different breeds, such as the American Shorthair, the British Shorthair, and the Chartreux, these are natural, sturdy cats with short coats — cats that have developed naturally in their respective countries of origin, without any exaggerations being made to their natural appearances. The American Shorthair, for example, looks very much like an average non-pedigree or moggy although in more refined colors. The British Shorthair is a fairly large cat with a rounded head, but without the short face seen in the Persian. The Chartreux is very similar to the British Shorthair. These cats all make ideal pets for those that want a pedigree cat but prefer one that is less delicate in build and looks than most others, and which has a steady temperament, without being either placid or overly energetic.

GOLDEN PERSIAN

The CHINCHILLA is one of the most popular of persians due to its beautiful coat, which can be either silver, golden, or pewter.

SEMI-LONGHAIR CATS

These again include many different breeds. Popular examples of Semi-Longhairs include the Maine Coon, the Birman, the Turkish Van, and the Ragdoll. Semi-Longhairs are longhaired cats, but unlike the Persian, these are not "true" Longhairs, and lack the very full coat of the Persian, which so easily mats and tangles. A Semi-Longhair cat will still need regular grooming, but much less so than a Persian, making these cats ideal for most people. They are also less placid and more playful than Persians, being rather similar in temperament to the Shorthair breeds. Some of these cats, in particular the Maine Coon and the Ragdoll, can grow very big — 20 pounds or more for an adult is not unusual.

SIAMESE CATS

This breed does not just include the Siamese, but also the Balinese, which is a semi-longhaired version of the Siamese, as well as the Colorpoint Shorthair and the Javanese. The latter two are color varieties of Siamese and Balinese that some registries do not recognize as actual Siamese or Balinese, although to all intents and purposes, the breeds are the same.

The Siamese, alongside the Persian, is the oldest breed of pedigree cat. Siamese have long, slender bodies with whip-like tails and large bat-like ears. The body is pale, with darker "points" coloring on face, ears, legs, and tail. These breeds are extremely intelligent, very vocal indeed, and far more energetic than most other breeds. A Siamese type cat is best suited to those that want a cat to interact with, as a Siamese will answer back when spoken to, and it will definitely not sit still for very long! This type of cat needs a lot of stimulation in the form of play (and preferably also a companion of their own kind) otherwise they easily get bored. In short, it is an extrovert cat, possibly best suited to a like-minded owner!

SIAMESE TORTISESHELL POINT

ORIENTAL CATS

These cats are, in essence, the same as Siamese. That is, they are Siamese-like cats of colors other than the traditional, Siamese ones. Oriental breeds include, for instance, the Oriental (both Shorthair and Longhair), and the Havana. Orientals can have many different colors; either being of all one color (as in the case of the Oriental Black or the Oriental White) or Tabby (such as the Oriental Brown Tabby or the Oriental Brown Spotted Tabby). In contrast, the Havana is always brown in color. The body and temperament of these cats are exactly the same as in the Siamese-type cats.

FOREIGN CATS

This group includes a large number of different breeds, such as the Abyssinian, the different Rex breeds (most commonly Cornish Rex and Devon Rex), the Russian Blue, the Ocicat, the Bengal, the Japanese Bobtail, the Turkish Angora, and the Sphynx. Cats of this type can vary greatly in looks — there are short-haired cats, longhaired cats, cats with no fur at all, cats with tails and cats without tails! Naturally, it is difficult to generalize about such a large variety of different cats, but very broadly speaking, Foreign type cats are somewhat similar to Siamese types in that they are intelligent, playful, and lively, although they are not quite as vocal and demanding as an actual Siamese.

Breed Classification

In the UK, cat breeds are divided into seven different breed groups, not dissimi-lar to the way in which most Kennel Clubs divide dog breeds into groups. In the US, however, most registries tend to classify the cat breeds simply into two different categories; Longhair or Shorthair.

Most US registries classify the various breeds exactly like this; those that have a short coat belong in the Shorthair breed group, and those with a long (or semi-long) coat belong in the Longhair group. Within the Cat Fanciers' Association (CFA), classification is, however, slightly more complicated. Longhaired breeds can be found in the Shorthair section — simply because a breed may first have been recognized as a Shorthair breed, and later when a Longhair version of that same breed is accepted, it will still stay in the Shorthair breed group. An exam-ple of this is the Scottish Fold, which was originally accepted as a Shorthair breed. When a Longhair version was recognized, it too was placed in the Shorthair group. Other registries choose to avoid this confusion, and either put each coat type of one breed into the appropriate group, or rename the new version. For example, some registries recognize the Longhair Scottish Fold as the Highland Fold.

In the UK, the seven different breed groups may at first look self-explanatory, but again there are exceptions to the basic rules. The UK recognized breeds tend to be placed in their respective groups according to looks and heritage, rather than length of coat or country of origin. Thus, the Exotic Shorthair belongs in the Longhair (Persian) breed group as it is a Persian in all senses except for the short coat. The Balinese belongs in the Siamese breed group as it is a longhaired

15

Siamese rather than a Semi-Longhair breed, and the Devon and Cornish Rexes, despite being native to Britain in origin, belong in the Foreign group due to their "foreign" looks!

The breed groups as accepted by the Governing Council of the Cat Fancy (GCCF — Britain's largest registry by far) are as follows:

LONGHAIR
This group includes all the Persian cats, divided into different color groups: Self, Tabby, Colourpoint, Smoke, Bicolor, Tortoiseshell, Tortie and White, Chinchilla, Shaded Silver, Pewter, Cameo, Golden. Persian cats are officially *not* called "Persian" by the GCCF, but simply "Longhair." As mentioned previously, the Exotic Shorthair also belongs in this group, due to their shared looks and common ancestry. Exotics are, at the moment, not divided into separate color groups.

SEMI-LONGHAIR
This is a group of longhaired cats that are not Persian Longhair. Their coats are not as full, do not mat as easily, and tend to lay flat on the body as opposed to having the "fluffed up" appearance of the Persian. The shape of the body and, in particular, the face, is very different, being more "natural" in looks in Semi-Longhair breeds. The Semi-Longhair breeds are: Birman, Turkish Van, Somali, Norwegian Forest Cat, and Maine Coon. Interestingly, the Somali was decided to belong in the Semi-Longhair group, despite the fact that it is a longhair version of the Abyssinian, which is in the Foreign group. The Ragdoll also belongs in this group, but is not yet fully recognized by the GCCF (see page 124).

SEAL BIRMAN

BLUE TABBY BIRMAN

BLUE BIRMAN

BRITISH
This group includes all the British Shorthairs of all the accepted colors, as well as the Manx.

FOREIGN
Foreign breeds are as mentioned earlier, not necessarily foreign in origin, but foreign in looks. That is, the cats tend to have slender bodies, pointed faces, and, often, large ears — although Foreign cats are not as exaggerated in looks as Siamese and Oriental cats. The Foreign breed group includes the following breeds: Russian Blue, Korat, Abyssinian, Cornish Rex, Devon Rex, Asian, and Burmilla. This breed group also includes several breeds that are not yet fully recognized by the GCCF (that is, the breed lacks Championship status, and no cat of these breeds can become Champion, or gain any other title). These breeds include color variations of recognized breeds, as well as Tiffanie, Tonkinese, Ocicat, Bengal, and Singapura.

BURMESE
This group includes all the color variations of the Burmese; Brown, Blue, Chocolate, Lilac, Red, Cream, and Tortoiseshells of various colors.

ORIENTAL
The Oriental breed group includes the Foreign White, Oriental Black, Havana, Oriental Lilac, Oriental Cinnamon, Oriental Red, Oriental Tortoiseshell, Oriental Tabby (of either spotted, classic, mackerel, or ticked pattern), and the Oriental Shaded. Oriental cats are essentially Siamese cats without the Siamese's pale body with colored points — for instance, an Oriental Black looks like an all-black Siamese.

SIAMESE
This group includes all of the 32 different color varieties of the Siamese, and the same colors of the Balinese.

Differences between the US and the UK

There are a large number of differences between the US cat scene and the corresponding UK one. The most obvious of these differences is the number of cat registries and organizations. In the UK, there is one main organization; the Governing Council of the Cat Fancy (GCCF), which recognizes breeds, registers kittens, and licenses shows. A good 95 percent of all pedigree cats are registered within this, although a second, much smaller organization, is also in existence, the Cat Association of Great Britain (CA), but this group is marginal.

In the US, however, there are no less than six major organizations, which each recognizes and registers cat breeds, establishes standards of points for each breed, sanctions shows, etc. Exactly which breeds of cats these six organizations recognize varies between the different groups, and occasionally even the name of a breed will differ — such as in the case of the Cream Point Siamese, which

LILAC TABBY TONKINESE

SCOTTISH FOLD WHITE

some registries accept as a color variety of the Siamese, but others classify as a separate breed; the Colorpoint Shorthair. Therefore, when a breed is described in this book, the relevant initials of the body or bodies that recognize that particular breed of cat are given. The registries and their initials are as follows:

American Association of Cat Enthusiasts (AACE)
American Cat Association (ACA)
American Cat Fanciers Association (ACFA)
Cat Fanciers Association (CFA)
Cat Fanciers Federation (CFF)
The International Cat Association (TICA)
Cat Association of Great Britain (CA)
Governing Council of the Cat Fancy (GCCF)

Between the US and the UK, there are also several differences in the way breeds look, and also in the names of the breeds. The Burmese, for instance, is so different in looks in the US and Europe, that some US registries recognize it as two separate breeds; Burmese and European Burmese. The Persian and Exotic have for many years shown a lot more type in the US than in the UK (that is, the cat has a shorter nose which gives it a flatter profile), mainly because this "extreme" (or "ultra") typed Persian and Exotic has been considered a fault in the GCCF's standard of points. UK breeders are, however, more and more starting to follow the trend set by Persian and Exotic breeders worldwide. An example of the confusion that can be caused by different names is apparent in the Himalayan, which is the Persian with Siamese coloring. This breed is known as the Colourpoint Longhair (or Persian) in most countries other than the US.

Many breeds that exist in the US, have not yet reached the UK. Typical examples of these include the Siberian, the American Shorthair, the American Wirehair, and the Japanese Bobtail. However, the UK bred Asian and Burmilla does not appear to have reached the US.

Whereas most US registries will recognize almost any breed of cat once established, the UK's GCCF refuses to recognize certain breeds on health grounds. The breeds currently refused recognition by the GCCF include the Sphynx, the Munchkin, and the Scottish Fold. The CA, however, tends to recognize any breeds that are recognized by the European body, Federation Interationale Feline (FIFe).

Shows and showing of pedigree cats also differ a lot between the two countries. In the US, cat shows are generally held over a weekend, with judging taking place on both days. The cats are shown in "judging rings," and each cat can be assessed by several different judges during the weekend. It may even be possible for a cat to attain a title such as Champion during just one weekend.

The cats judged in each ring are placed in order of the judge's preference, and the best ones go forward to the final. To gain titles such as Champion, Grand Champion, Premier, and Grand Premier ("Premier" being the neutered cat's equivalent title of Champion), the cat has to gain points by reaching finals in the various rings. The cats' owners are allowed to personally carry their cats to the judging table, and to watch the judging in progress, and the judge will give a running commentary to his or her audience. When a cat is not in the judging ring, it is penned, and each pen is decorated as seen fit by the owner, although most rules state that the sides, top, and back of the pen have to be covered, for which purpose most owners use special show drapes. The pens can be very lavishly decorated indeed, with each serving as a sort of advert for the breeder.

In the UK, under the GCCF, shows are run in a very different way. Cats can only be shown once every 14 days, as there must be a clear 13 days in between each show, to minimize the risk of infection being spread. This rule applies to all cats owned by one person/cattery, it is not possible to show one cat one week, and another the next. Accordingly, all GCCF shows are one day events. Before even being allowed inside the hall, each cat entered into a GCCF show will be examined by a veterinary surgeon to ensure that it is fit and healthy. The cats must be kept in pens that are all identically furnished in white, with no drapes allowed. The judges walk between the pens with a table on wheels, removing each cat from its pen and assessing it on the table. Thus the need for the cat to be moved from one part of the hall to another is eliminated.

While judging is in progress, no exhibitors are allowed inside the hall. Each cat enters into only one main class (the open class), and to gain the title of Champion, will need to be awarded three Challenge Certificates (CCs), by three different judges, on three different occasions.

Finally, veterinary practices also differ between the US and the UK. In the UK, declawing of cats is never done (I would strongly advise against this practice), and unlike in the US, cat breeders are not able to personally purchase vaccines and other medications to treat their cats themselves — everything has to be done through a veterinary surgeon, with proof of vaccination being required at shows, boarding catteries etc.

Crossbreeding and Moggies

The purposeful crossbreeding of cats, and the indiscriminate breeding of moggies, are two very different subjects.

To create new pedigree breeds, existing pedigree cats are on occasion mated to each other. The offspring can be registered as crossbreeds or as an experimental breed. Several new breeds have been created in this way, such as the Exotic Shorthair, which was a cross between the Persian and the American Shorthair in the US, and between the Persian and the British Shorthair in the UK. The Tonkinese was a cross between a Siamese and a Burmese, and the Burmilla, started off as a cross between a Chinchilla Persian and a Burmese.

To create a new breed is a major undertaking which demands a lot of genetic knowledge, and space for a lot of cats, as well as a lot of suitable homes for all the pet kittens that are produced in the process, as not all will be suitable for further breeding. It is not a project that anybody can undertake, and it is never a good idea to set out to create a new breed without first having carefully thought through and researched the project. However, most breeds come about as natural mutations, rather than being created. All the Rex breeds, for instance, occurred naturally in moggy litters, in various places in the world. The first one, the Cornish Rex, was a rex-coated kitten born to an ordinary farm cat mother in Cornwall, England. Many other breeds have come about in similar ways, where breeders have seized the opportunity to create a breed by using new mutations.

Moggies, on the other hand, are your average farm cats or alley cats — they are mongrels; cats without pedigrees, or particular looks. A moggy can look like anything, and all over the world moggies are by far the most common type of cat to be kept as pets.

Much can be said about moggies. It is generally believed that they are healthier and have a longer life span than pedigree cats. This is rather a sweeping generalization, as health and longevity naturally vary between different individuals, and also between different bloodlines. However, it is true to say that moggies are usually very hardy creatures that fight off disease easier than many pedigree cats, though this doesn't mean that they cannot succumb to those diseases. Moggies do tend to be long-lived, with many reaching 15 or even 20 years of age, but at the same time, some pedigree breeds live for just as long, with the Siamese, for instance, having a reputation as particularly long-lived. So, any prospective cat owner choosing between a pedigree or a moggy, should not make a decision based on health or stamina. Instead consider what sort of cat you want, and why. With pedigree cats, it is possible to predict what sort of

TONKINESE

temperament, coat, and size they will have once adult, while with a moggy kitten nobody will know! Most moggies make excellent pets, they simply are not as predictable as pedigree cats.

What must be stressed very strongly, is that moggies should *not* be bred. The world is full of moggies. Every single day, all over the world, thousands of them are being put to sleep, simply because they are unwanted. There are not enough homes for all moggies, as far too many are born. The responsible moggy owner will have his or her pet neutered, to prevent any kittens from being born. The neutered cat will become a loving pet, and will never miss the experience of giving birth, or fathering kittens. There is absolutely no truth in the old wives' tale that a cat should be allowed to have at least one litter before being neutered. If all female cats were bred from just once, there would be even more unwanted cats in the world having to be put to sleep. A female cat that has had a litter, may actually miss being able to have more kittens after she has been neutered. If she has never had a litter, she will be none the wiser and will be a happy, content pet. The male cat will be a lot less likely to stray, to get into fights with other cats (and so less likely to catch fatal diseases), and also less likely to spray urine both indoors and outdoors, which almost all entire males do as a form of territorial scent marking.

Moggy owners sometimes argue that they want to breed one litter from their female, and that it will not create any unwanted kittens, as they intend to keep one for themseleves, and have several friends that have promised to take a kitten each. This may well be the case, but surely, if you know several people that would wish to give a home to a kitten, it would be a much better deed if all these people instead went to visit their local cat shelter or rescue home, and gave a home to a rescued cat that might otherwise be put to sleep? These cats are in desperate need of good homes, and, as there will never be enough, it is irresponsible to deliberately create more moggies.

Finally, to those that still think it might be a good idea to breed moggy kittens; consider the costs involved. To be able to bring up a litter in a responsible way, you will first need to blood test both the male and the female cat, to ensure that they do not carry Feline Leukaemia Virus (FeLV), or Feline Immunodeficiency Virus (FIV) — both incurable, fatal diseases which can be spread by mating, and which can be carried by an asymptomatic cat for years. The kittens need to stay with their mother for 12 weeks, and both the kittens and their mother will need a lot of nutritious food — the female (queen) will need a lot more food than when she isn't pregnant or lactating. The kittens will also need worming, and by the time they are ready to go to their new homes aged 12 weeks, they should be fully vaccinated. All of this involves a lot of money and, as the kittens are moggies and not pedigrees, people are not likely to want to part with large sums of money (when they can get a free kitten from the neighbor down the road who has cut corners and reared a litter full of fleas, worms, earmites, and infections, given away before they are fully weaned) and so you may end up having to keep all the kittens yourself.

Be responsible. Neuter your moggies.

CAT BREEDS

Abyssinian

AACE, ACA, ACFA, CFA, CFF, TICA, GCCF, CA

Origin: The Abyssinian is a very old breed, possibly counting the Egyptian Hunting Cat as one if its ancestors. The exact origin of the breed remains unknown, but a cat closely resembling an Abyssinian in looks was brought into Great Britain in 1868 by Mrs Barrett-Lennard, who was the wife of a sea captain. The cat, named "Zulu," was pictured in a book published in 1874. It is further believed that the breed has an African connection, as it resembles the African Sand Cat. There are records of Abyssinians dating back as far as 1892, and the breed has been registered in Britain with the GCCF since the organizations very beginnings in 1910.

Description: The Abyssinian is a medium sized cat of Foreign type. It is shorthaired, with a ticked agouti coat (this means that it is a tabby without any stripes or spots). It is a slender cat with large ears and a long face, but not as much as in many Oriental breeds. The cat must not be too cobby or solid, yet should be muscular in appearance. The body should be heavy, but the Abyssinian must never be too fat, as a large stomach will greatly ruin the outline of the elegant

body. The ears have tufts on the tips, rather like a lynx, which of course also has a similar ticked color.

Colors: For many years, there were only two colors accepted in the Abyssinian, although other colors had appeared from time to time during many years — Ruddy (known as Usual in the UK) and Sorrel (red). The usual color has a ruddy orange to apricot-colored background, which is evenly ticked with black. There must be no stripes, bars, or spots visible at all. There is a darker line of ticking along the spine of the cat out to the tip of the tail, and the tips of the ears are dark. The only evident tabby-markings are to be found on the Abyssinian's forehead. If inspected closely, each individual hair is divided into four sections. The Sorrel is much redder in appearance, and the black ticking is less obvious, but must still be present. These days, several other colors have been developed, although those which are fully acceptable vary between the different cat registries. The new colors include the Blue, Chocolate, Lilac, Fawn, Red (different to the Sorrel), the Cream, and then the various colors in Silver — which means that the cat has a white under-coat with top color, which gives a shining silver appearance.

Temperament: The Abyssinian is an intelligent, outgoing breed which loves attention. These cats are playful and love adventures, and can work out the most incredible tasks, such as how to open doors or cupboards. They are vocal yet not noisy, and tend to attach themself to just one or a few persons, and then stay loyal to them. Many people find them the ideal pet cat, as they are also hardy and less delicate looking than Oriental breeds, yet still very lithe and elegant, with a great zest for life.

American Bobtail

ACFA, TICA

Origin: The American Bobtail came about as a natural mutation in an ordinary litter of moggy kittens. The first Bobtail kitten was found in an American Indian reservation in Arizona, and was acquired from there by John and Brenda Sanders from Iowa. They started breeding for the Bobtailed look, and the breed was eventually granted recognition by TICA in 1989.

Description: The American Bobtail can be either shorthaired or semi-long-haired. The cat is of medium size, and should be muscular and well-fleshed, but not fat. The head has oval shaped eyes under a heavy brow, which gives it the look of a hunting cat. The coat in the Semi-Longhair should be shaggy look-ing, and both coat varieties should be dense and water resistant. The tail is the most obvious feature of the American Bobtail; this is short and should stand erect. The tail reaches approximately halfway to the cat's hocks. It is important to breed from cats with good hips, as cats with no tail or a very short tail may, at times, suffer from congenital hip defects.

Colors: All colors and patterns are acceptable.

Temperament: The American Bobtail is friendly and curious, but can be rather shy with strangers. An altogether natural cat, the American Bobtail shows no exaggerations in its temperament; it is placid yet playful, not overly energetic nor lazy. It is a quiet cat, very seldom using its voice. It is important that the cat has a wild look, but not a wild temperament.

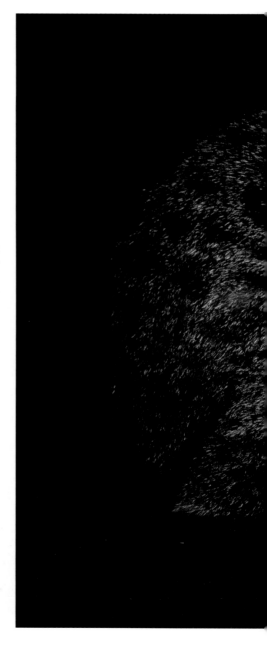

American Curl

AACE, ACA, ACFA, CFA, CFF, TICA

Origin: The first American Curl appeared in 1981, in California. The longhaired black kitten, which had unusual ears that were curled backwards, suddenly turned up at the doorstep of Joe and Grace Ruga. After some initial resistance, the Rugas decided to keep the kitten, which they called "Shulamith." Six months later, she gave birth to a litter of four kittens. Two of these kittens had the same curled back ears as their mother. The Rugas contacted a geneticist, who told them that the curled ears were a new genetic mutation, and obviously a dominant trait as just one parent with curled ears was needed for kittens with curled ears to be born. It was, however, not until two years later, in 1983, that cat fanciers started to breed selectively for these unusual ears.

Description: The American Curl can be either shorthaired or semi-long-haired, due to the fact that the original cats were of mixed ancestry and so threw both longhair and shorthair

kittens when bred. It is a medium sized breed, which should look elegant and graceful. The head is fairly long, with large, walnut shaped eyes. The body is medium in every sense, without any exaggerations — this is a natural looking cat. The ears are, of course, the most striking feature of the American Curl. As in the case of the Scottish Fold, which has its ears folded down rather than back like the American Curl, straight eared kittens are also born, and these are used for breeding. The curled back ears are measured according to how curled they are; a first degree curl is just a slight curl at the very tip of the ears, and these cats are not shown or bred from. A second degree curl is a cat whose ears curl backwards at between 45 to 90 degrees, and these cats are not considered worthy of showing either. The show quality American Curl has a third degree curl which is from 90 to 180 degrees, with the tips pointing towards the center of the base of the skull, but not touching the back of the head.

Colors: Any coat color or pattern is acceptable in this breed.

Temperament: The American Curl is a friendly and curious cat, which likes to be involved in whatever goes on in the household. It is intelligent, and retains its kitten-like playfulness for all of its life. The American Curl is not a very vocal cat, although it does use its voice when it feels that there is a real need to do so. This is a sociable breed that gets on well with other cats and dogs.

American Shorthair

AACE, ACA, ACFA, CFA, CFF, TICA

Origin: The American Shorthair is an entirely natural looking cat, rather like a pedigree moggy. It is believed that the ancestors of the American Shorthair came to North America with the early pioneers from Europe; there are old records which state that there were several cats onboard the ship *Mayflower*. The cats were no doubt brought along as a means to keep vermin at bay, as any rats on a ship could both spread disease and eat into the food supplies needed for the humans. Once the foreign breeds of pedigree cat started to arrive in the US, the popularity of the American Shorthair started to decline, as people tended to favor the more exotic breeds such as Siamese and Persians. Also,

the native American Shorthair would mix freely with these cats, and so the bloodlines quickly became diluted. Eventually, breeders interested in the American Shorthair decided to preserve the breed for the future, and so set up a breeding program. The American Shorthair was one of the first five breeds to be recognized by the CFA.

Description: The American Shorthair should truly resemble a "working" cat, one that easily could go out and catch rats and mice — it is a natural looking cat without any exaggerations. The size is medium to large, and the cat is strongly built and powerful. The head is large, with full cheeks, giving a somewhat square impression. The ears are of medium size with slightly rounded tips and the eyes are large and almond shaped. The coat is short and dense, and not as sleek as some other Shorthair breeds, this is simply due to its thickness; it is meant to be water resistant.

Colors: The American Shorthair comes in over 80 different colors and the only color not acceptable is the pointed Siamese pattern. Most commonly seen is the Silver Tabby.

Temperament: The American Shorthair is quiet, gentle, and very friendly. It is usually a very steady cat which is reliable with children, and which easily makes friends with other cats and dogs. Not overly energetic nor too placid, the American Shorthair is the epitome of the common domestic cat, yet in a pedigree package.

American Wirehair

ACA, ACFA, CFA, TICA

Origin: The American Wirehair first appeared as a spontaneous mutation in 1961. The first Wirehair kitten to be born was grandly known as "Council Rock Farm Adams of Hi-Fi," and he was born to two perfectly ordinary farm cats in New York. The American Wirehair has been bred ever since, although the breed is relatively unknown outside the US, and this particular Rex mutation has never occured elsewhere. The wirehair is a dominant gene, so just one wirehaired parent is needed for Wirehair kittens to be born, although to gain the best possible coat for showing, two Wirehair parents are preferred. The breed was first recognized in 1967.

Description: The American Wirehair is of medium to large size, without any exaggerations, unlike most other rex-coated breeds. The body is similar to that of the American Shorthair and the head should be in proportion to the body, with prominent cheek bones and a well-developed muzzle. The ears are of medium size with slightly rounded tips and are set well apart. The eyes are large and round. The legs are medium in length, and the cat should be well muscled. The coat is naturally the most obvious feature of the American Wirehair, and this should be very tightly waved and feel springy to the touch. The American Wirehair is quite unlike most other cats with rex coats, its fur being more wavy than curly, and harsh rather than soft. The whiskers are curly.

Colors: White, with either blue, gold, or odd eyes (that is, one eye of each color), Black, Blue, Red, Cream, Chinchilla Silver, Shaded Silver, Shell Cameo (Red Chinchilla), Shaded Cameo (Red Shaded), Black Smoke, Blue Smoke, Cameo Smoke, Classic Tabby pattern and Mackerel Tabby pattern in Silver, Red, Brown, Blue, Cream, or Cameo, Tortoiseshell, Calico, dilute Calico, Blue-Cream, or Bicolor. Other occuring colors are acceptable, except for Chocolate, Lilac, or Himalayan.

Temperament: The American Wirehair is described as a friendly cat, but one which is quiet and somewhat reserved, preferring to attach itself to one particular person, and not being overly enthusiastic when it comes to greeting strangers.

Asian

GCCF

Origin: The Asian breed really comprises several different breeds of cat, with the Burmilla being the best known. As the Burmilla was created, other colors and coat lengths also developed, and these were to become the different types of Asian cat.

The breeds came about as a mistake. Well-known cat fancier, Baroness Miranda von Kirchberg, a breeder of Chinchilla Persians and Burmese cats, had a litter born by accident in 1981. She owned two kittens of different breeds, but which had become very close friends. This was a Chinchilla male by the name of "Jemari Sanquist," and a Burmese female, "Bambino Lilac Faberge," a Lilac. Once "Faberge" started calling, it naturally became necessary to separate the two cats. As the Baroness was very busy, one day she simply put "Faberge" inside her study, shut the

door, and left the house. When her housekeeper later found the male Chinchilla crying outside the door, and the Burmese queen crying on the inside, she assumed that the pair had been separated and opened the door. Needless to say, the cats mated, and a litter resulted. The litter consisted of four kittens, all of Burmese type but with the Black Tipped coloring of the Chinchilla. The Baroness realized what potential this new type of cat had, as not only was it attractive but it also had an excellent temperament and hybrid vigor. Accordingly, in 1982, a new breeding program was started, in consultation with the Burmese breed clubs. The aim was to create a cat which was essentially a Burmese in looks, but with the Silver coloring of the Chinchilla.

Eventually, the other colors were added to the breeding program.

Description: The Asian cats are essentially Burmese cats of colors other than those accepted in the Burmese. The Asian group includes the Burmilla, which is, essentially, a Shaded Silver colored Burmese, the Asian Smoke, which is a non-agouti silvered cat, the Asian Tabby, the Asian Selfs, which include the Bombay, one of these breeds to actually be known outside the UK, and finally the Tiffanie, which is the semi-longhair of the group. The aim of all the breeds is to produce a Burmese type cat, but with different colors.

Colors: The Asian Tabby comes in either Ticked, Mackerel, Spotted or Classic Tabby pattern, in either Silver or Standard, of many different colors. The Burmilla is basically a shaded cat,

which also comes in different colors. The Asian Self can have various colors, of which the Black Bombay is the best known. The Asian Smoke may have several different colors too. The Tiffanie is the semi-longhair Asian, and this cat can have any color or pattern.

Temperament: All of the Asian cats are very friendly and outgoing, with excellent temperaments. They are lively and playful, with a great curiosity. The Asian cat loves company, be it either human or feline, and does not like to be left on its own for very long. This is a cat that will be very devoted to its owner, in a rather dog-like way, and they will often choose one person as their most special friend. They also get on well with other cats and dogs.

39

Balinese

AACE, ACA, ACFA, CFA, CFF, TICA, GCCF, CA

Origin: The Balinese is, to all intents and purposes, a longhaired version of the Siamese, and it is believed to have come about as a natural mutation. During the 1940s, longhaired kittens were occasionally born in Siamese litters bred in the US. Some breeders decided that they liked the look of this cat, and so continued to breed the longhaired kittens together. The long-haired Siamese was found to breed true, i.e. when two longhairs were mated together, they would produce a litter of all longhaired Siamese kittens, and by the 1950s such matings became more common. By the late 1950s the CFF had become the first registering body to accept this as a new breed of cat, and the name Balinese was decided upon — after the graceful dancers of Bali. Later, the breed was imported into the UK where, as there was such a small gene pool, the Balinese breed has been out-crossed to Siamese from time to time. Despite being a very attractive cat the Balinese has remained a much less popular breed than the Siamese.

Description: The Balinese is a true Siamese in all but coat, which is semi-long. On the body, the fur lays flat, with a larger ruff on the chest which tends to be fuller during colder weather. The tail is the most striking feature of the Balinese as there the coat is at its fullest. In every other respect, the Balinese has the same looks as the Siamese, with the long, svelte, and elegantly slender body, a long wedge shaped face, tall, pricked ears, long slender legs, and vividly blue eyes.

Colors: The Balinese comes in the same colors as the Siamese, although as in the case of the Siamese, some registering bodies only accept the four classic colors as true Balinese colors; Seal Point, Blue Point, Chocolate Point, and Lilac Point. The remaining colors are then referred to as Javanese, and not Balinese.

The basic Balinese colorings are: Seal Point, Blue Point, Chocolate Point, Lilac Point, Flame Point (Red Point outside the US), Cream Point, Seal Tortie Point, Blue Tortie Point, Chocolate Tortie Point, Lilac Tortie Point, Cinnamon Point, Caramel Point, Fawn Point, Cinnamon Tortie Point, Caramel Tortie Point, Fawn Tortie Point. To these 16 colors can then also be added Lynx Point (known as Tabby Point outside the US) — that is, the color is broken up by tabby markings, so that the tail and legs are striped, and the face shows the classical tabby markings with the "M" on the forehead.

Temperament: The Balinese is an extrovert, no doubt about it. Extremely intelligent, energetic, lively, and playful, it loves jumping and climbing. This cat will easily learn how to open doors, and will like nothing more than getting up to mischief. The Balinese is a very single minded cat, dominant in temperament, which will go through with whatever he or she has decided to do; there is no stopping a determined Balinese! A very vocal cat, the Balinese will talk to you, answer back every time it is spoken to, and if it does not get his own way or wants an early dinner, it will yell at its owner in a very loud voice indeed. Balinese tend to be very devoted to their particular owner, but may find it hard to accept strangers. The Balinese does not like to be left on its own, and is happier being kept in the company of other cats, in particular cats of the same or a similar breed, as at times Balinese may find it difficult to get on with breeds of cats that are markedly different to its own temperament.

41

Bengal

ACA, ACFA, CFF, TICA, GCCF, CA

Origin: The Bengal came about by deliberate crosses between Asian Leopard Cats and ordinary domestic pet cats. Breeders in the US wanted to create a truly wild-looking domestic cat with the spectacular coat of the Leopard Cat. Today, most Bengals have a very minor percentage of wild blood in their genetic make up, and as such are not much different from other domestic cats, apart from in looks. Crosses to Leopard Cats are, however, still being done and it is recommended that the first, second, and even third generation crosses from wild cats should not be exhibited. These may also be unsuitable as pets, as they are too wild in their behavior.

Description: The Bengal is a large and very muscular cat, in order that it looks as much as possible like a true wild cat. It is sleek and powerful, with the hind legs being slightly longer than the front legs. The head is broad and slightly rounded, of medium length. The ears are small or medium in size, with rounded tips. What makes the

Bengal stand out from other breeds is its coat coloring. The coat is always spotted or marble tabby and it is very thick, feeling extremely soft. The markings are clear, and much better defined than in ordinary tabby cats, and the spotteds show larger spots. The coat has the effect of gold dust having been sprinkled over it, giving it an almost satin appearance, referred to as glitter.

Colors: The Bengal comes as Brown Marbled, Snow Marbled (with either blue or any other color eyes), Brown Spotted, and Snow Spotted.

Temperament: The Bengal should have a reliable temper and must not exhibit any undesirable wild traits. It is a confident and highly intelligent cat which at its best is very friendly. The Bengal talks in a voice different to that of other domestic cats, sounding more like the Asian Leopard Cat. The overall impression of the Bengal should be that it is in fact a miniature leopard.

Birman

ACA, ACFA, CFA, CFF, TICA, GCCF, CA

Origin: The entire history of the Birman's origin is not fully known, but it is believed that the breed descends from the same genetic mutation that the Siamese was developed from, and that it originates from somewhere in the southeast Asian area. The name of the Birman comes from the French *sacre de Birmanie* (the sacred cat of Burma). There is a centuries old legend surrounding the Birman cat, which strives to explain its unusual looks. Birman cats, then pure white, were supposedly kept in the Buddhist temples of Burma. In one of them, the temple of Lao-Tsun, a statue of a golden goddess with blue eyes was kept. One of the temple's priests, Mun-Ha, often knelt in front of the goddess in prayer. The temple also housed a white cat, "Sinh," which was always at the side of Mun-Ha. One night, just as Mun-Ha was kneeling in front of the goddess, he was killed in a raid on the temple. At the precise moment of death, "Sinh" stepped onto Mun-Ha's body, and gazed at the golden goddess. Immediately, or so the legend says, "Sinh's" eyes became the same blue color as the eyes of the golden goddess, the white legs became golden brown, but where Sinh's paws rested on his dead master, they remained white, showing their purity.

The Birman cat eventually made it to France in 1919, brought from Burma as a gift to two men that had helped protect Buddhist priests from raids and attacks by an opposing religion. It was not until the 1960s, however, that the breed started to spread to other countries.

Description: The Birman is a medium sized, semi-longhaired cat that is natural looking, with a medium length face and average body. A cat of striking beauty, with its contrasts of colors, it is perhaps little wonder that the Birman today is immensely popular. The semi-long coat is silky, yet requires little grooming.

Colors: The original Birman cat was Seal Point, as described in the legend. These days, Seal Point is still the most popular color, alongside the diluted version of Seal — the Blue Point. But the Birman now comes in all the same colors as the Himalayan cat. There are ten basic colors; Seal Point, Blue Point, Chocolate Point, Lilac Point, Cream Point, Flame Point (Red Point

in the UK), Seal Tortie Point, Blue-Cream Point, Chocolate Tortie Point, and Lilac-Cream Point, and these ten colors then come in Lynx Points too (known as Tabby Points in the UK), with stripes showing on the legs and face, and a ringed tail. The Birman's body is pale, with darker points coloring the face, ears, legs, and tail. The front paws show white gloves, with the hind paws having larger white gauntlets. The eyes are a vivid blue.

Temperament: The Birman has a sweet and playful temperament, it is neither too laid back nor too energetic, but rather somewhere in between. Birmans get very attached to their owners, and remain playful for all of their lives. They enjoy a rest on their owner's lap, but the next moment will be alert and ready for a game. Birmans get on with most other breeds of cat, as well as other pets.

Bombay

ACA, ACFA, CFA, CFF, TICA, GCCF

Origin: The Bombay was created in the late 1950s in the US by breeder Nikki Horner. Originally, her wish was to create a black version of the Burmese, so she crossed a Brown Burmese with a Black American Shorthair. The kittens that resulted reminded her very much of miniature panthers, and so she decided to abandon the project of trying to breed black Burmese, and instead concentrated on this new breed that she had before her, which she decided to call Bombay. The CFA recognized the breed in 1976, with other registries following later.

In the UK, the same breed developed independently several years later, but here it came as a result of an ordinary black non-pedigree moggy having mated two Burmese queens, one brown and one blue, belonging to a Mrs B. Oliver. The resulting kittens became the foundation for the Bombay breed in the UK.

Colors: Black only.

Description: The Bombay is similar in build to the Burmese, and in the UK it is classified as one of the Asian breeds; cats of Burmese type but of colors

other than the recognized Burmese colors. This is a cat which is neither as sleek as the Siamese, nor as rounded as the British or American Shorthairs; it is somewhere in between with a wedge shaped head of shorter length than a Siamese. The ears are medium to large. Any tendency to look like a Siamese or Oriental in body shape is considered a serious fault, as is cobbyness.

The Bombay is a medium sized cat with a short, dense, and sleek coat. The color is jet black, with eyes that are various shades of yellow or green. The Bombay should look like a miniature panther, and so the shining, jet black coat is its most prominent feature.

Temperament: The Bombay is very similar in temperament to its ancestor the Burmese, but is perhaps slightly less active, probably due to the non-Burmese cats in its genetic make-up. All the same, it is a playful breed, a mischievous cat with a large amount of curiosity. Not as vocal as the Siamese, yet more talkative than a Persian or moggy, the Bombay lets you

know that he is there! Bombays can be very people oriented cats, they crave company and do not like to be ignored. Having two as opposed to one will double the fun, and will also give the Bombay a much needed sparring partner in games of rough and tumble.

British Shorthair

AACE, ACA, ACFA, CFA, CFF, TICA, GCCF, CA

Origin: The British Shorthair is exactly what it sounds like; a shorthaired cat which originated in Great Britain. Developed from ordinary moggies and refined for more than a century, the British could perhaps be described as the pedigree version of the ordinary moggy. It has been a recognized breed in the UK since the very beginning of the cat fancy.

Description: The British Shorthair no longer looks quite like your average moggy. During the years, breeders have worked hard to improve its looks and thus the British Shorthair is a large cat with a round, massive head — yet without the short nose seen in the Persian and Exotic. The eyes are large and round, the tail has a rounded tip and is thick-set. The coat is short, and much more dense than in most moggies.

Colors: To many, a British Shorthair equals the British Blue. Self Blue is the color that steadily has remained the most popular in the British Shorthair, even though there now exists a virtual rainbow of colors within the breed. Which colors that are fully recognized varies between the different cat registries; some, for instance, do not accept the British as a Colorpointed breed (i.e. Siamese colored). The following colors and markings can be found in the British Shorthair:

Self colors (solid): White (either with blue, orange, or odd eyes), Black, Chocolate, Lilac, Red, Blue, Cream.

Bicolor: Colored cat with white markings; either Black, Blue, Chocolate, Lilac, Red, or Cream.

Tabby: Can be either Classic Tabby pattern, Mackerel, or Spotted Tabby, as well as Tortie Tabbies (Torbies). The tabby colors include Silver Tabby, Blue Silver Tabby, Chocolate Silver Tabby, Lilac Silver Tabby, Red Silver Tabby, Cream Silver Tabby, Red Tabby, Brown Tabby, Blue Tabby, Chocolate Tabby, Lilac Tabby, Cream Tabby, Tortie Tabby, Tortie Silver Tabby.

Tortoiseshell: Tortoiseshell, Blue Cream, Chocolate Tortie, and Lilac Tortie are acceptable, as are the same colors with white markings — known as Tortoiseshell and White in the UK, Calico in the US.

Tipped: The Tipped British Shorthair is a white cat with colored tips to each hair; basically, this is the shorthaired version of the Chinchilla Persian. Most commonly seen is the Black Tipped (same color as a Chinchilla Persian), but others include Blue Tipped, Chocolate Tipped, Lilac Tipped, Red Tipped, Cream Tipped, Black Tortie Tipped, Blue Tortie Tipped, Chocolate Tortie Tipped, Lilac Tortie Tipped, and finally the Golden Tipped, which is the British version of the apricot-colored Golden Persian.

Smoke: The Smoke is a silver color without tabby markings; the top coat is colored, with the undercoat white. The Smoke British Shorthair comes in Black Smoke, Blue Smoke, Chocolate Smoke, Lilac Smoke, Red Smoke, Cream Smoke, Tortie Smoke, Blue

Tortie Smoke, Chocolate Tortie Smoke, and Lilac Tortie Smoke.

Colorpointed: The Colorpointed British Shorthair is a British cat with Siamese markings and blue eyes; a pale coated cat with darker points on face, ears, legs, and tail. Points can be Seal, Blue, Chocolate, Lilac, Red, Cream, Seal Tortie, Blue-Cream, Chocolate Tortie, Lilac Tortie, Seal Tabby, Blue Tabby, Chocolate Tabby, Lilac Tabby, Red Tabby, Cream Tabby, Seal Tortie Tabby, Blue-Cream Tabby, Chocolate Tortie Tabby, Lilac Tortie Tabby, Seal Smoke, Blue Smoke, Chocolate Smoke, Lilac Smoke, Red Smoke, Cream Smoke, Tortie Smoke, Silver Tabby, Blue Silver Tabby, Chocolate Silver Tabby, Lilac Silver Tabby, Red Silver Tabby, Cream Silver Tabby, Seal Tortie Silver Tabby, Blue Tortie Silver Tabby, Chocolate Tortie Silver Tabby, Lilac Tortie Silver Tabby.

Temperament: The British Shorthair is a friendly, good natured cat with a placid, laid back temperament. Some people would go as far as to call them lazy, as the British loves nothing more than a quiet doze in front of the fire. They are steady and without a hint of nervousness. The British loves his or her food, and often has a tendency to put on weight once adult, as it is not a particularly energetic or playful cat. Some British are lap cats that happily will spend hours on their owner's lap; others prefer to sleep in their own chosen spot.

Burmese

AACE, ACA, ACFA, CFA, CFF, TICA, GCCF, CA

Origin: The Burmese originates from Thailand (then known as Siam), just like the Siamese and the Birman cat. Legends tell of Burmese cats being kept in monasteries in Burma, and the breed was mentioned in Thai books cenuries ago. The first Burmese to be imported into the US was a brown queen by the name of "Wong Mau." This was in 1920. She was mated to a Siamese, and became the founder of the entire breed, although later imports were made. The breed eventually reached the UK later during the century.

These days, there is a large difference in looks between the US and the UK Burmese, so much so that some US registries even accept them as two different breeds; Burmese and European Burmese. The US Burmese has sadly suffered from many health problems, and as such the GCCF has banned any imported Burmese from being introduced into UK pedigrees. The Burmese is so popular in the UK that it has its own breed group.

Description: The Burmese is a cat of Foreign type, a slender and elegant cat, but not as slim as the Oriental. The head is more rounded than that of the Siamese, the ears are medium sized with rounded tips, and, unlike in the Siamese and Oriental, the head has a nose break. The Burmese is a medium sized cat with a muscular body that should feel heavy. The coat is short, close laying, and very glossy. In the US, the Burmese has a more square head than in the UK and the rest of the world, and the Brown Burmese shows a darker coloring.

Colors: Eye color is any shade of yellow in all colors. The most popular color of the Burmese is the Brown, which is a rich seal brown. There are also Blue, Chocolate, Lilac, Red, Brown Tortie, Cream, Blue Tortie, Chocolate Tortie, and Lilac Tortie Burmese.

Temperament: The Burmese is a true family cat — loving, friendly, and playful. It is also a very active breed, always ready for a game. Burmese cats are very curious and like to be involved in whatever their owners are doing. They will happily follow you around the house, checking out everything that is going on, slinking inside open cupboards, watching the water running from the tap in the kitchen or bathroom, anything at all is of interest to a Burmese. The Burmese is not a cat for those who want a quiet lap cat, as they are energetic and vocal, and easily get bored if they are not allowed to take part in the various daily activities of a household. However, Burmese are also very affectionate cats, and will, at times, happily settle down on anybody's lap as soon as that person sits down. They love company so much that they cannot bear to be left alone for long periods at a time, so for owners that are out during large parts of the day, it is a wise choice to purchase two Burmese that can keep each other amused, rather than keep a single cat which will get bored.

Burmilla

GCCF, CA

Origin: The Burmilla is part of the Asian breed group, which is little known outside the UK. The Burmilla was the first of the Asian cats to be bred, and the breed came about as a complete accident.

Well known cat fancier, Baroness Miranda von Kirchberg, a breeder of Chinchilla Persians and Burmese cats, had a litter born in 1981. She owned two cats which were of different breeds, but which had become very close friends. This was a Chinchilla male by the name of "Jemari Sanquist," and a Burmese female, "Bambino Lilac Faberge," a Lilac. Once "Faberge" started calling it naturally became necessary to separate the two cats. As the Baroness was very busy, one day she simply put "Faberge" inside her study, shut the door, and left the house. When her

Description: The Burmilla is a Burmese type cat with silver coloring. It has a short sleek coat, is of medium size, and has a medium wedge head.

Colors: Either Tipped or Shaded in Black, Blue, Chocolate, Lilac, Red, Caramel, Apricot, Black Tortie, Cream, Blue Tortie, Chocolate Tortie, Lilac Tortie, or Caramel Tortie.

Temperament: The Burmilla is an intelligent and affectionate cat. Outgoing and active, it loves to play, and has a curiosity for everything. Many Burmillas like to perch on their owner's shoulders, and they love jumping and climbing.

housekeeper later found the male Chinchilla crying outside the door, and the Burmese queen crying on the inside, she assumed that they had been accidentally separated — and opened the door. The cats mated, and a litter resulted, which consisted of four kittens, all of Burmese type but with the black tipped coloring of the Chinchilla. The Baroness realized what a potential this new type of cat had, as not only was it attractive, it also had an excellent temperament and hybrid vigor. In 1982, a breeding program was started, in consultation with the Burmese breed clubs. The aim was to create a cat which was essentially Burmese in looks, but with the Silver coloring of the Chinchilla.

Chantilly

AACE, ACFA

Origin: The Chantilly breed originates from a pair of chocolate colored semi-longhaired cats of Foreign type, that were purchased by cat fancier Jennie Robinson from New York in 1967. The two kittens, named "Thomas" and "Shirley," had an unknown background. In fact, the kittens were being sold as part of an estate sale. "Shirley" eventually gave birth to a litter in 1969, which consisted of six kittens which were all identical to their parents. Jennie Robinson then embarked upon a beeding program to further this new breed of cat, and during the 1970s, "Thomas," "Shirley," and several of their offspring were registered by the ACA as Foreign Longhairs. It was believed by some that these cats may have had Burmese ancestry, but many factors spoke against this view. No Burmese cats have ever knowingly been mixed into this breed.

Burmese breeder Sigyn Lund, from Florida, purchased some of Jennie Robinson's cats, and it was she who decided to call the new breed Tiffany, rather than Foreign Longhair. She preferred this name as it seemed more "classy." However, the ACA eventually dropped the breed from its register as it was so rare.

At the very same time as the Foreign Longhair/Tiffany was being developed in the US, the same breed had occured naturally in Canada. These cats were eventually used for breeding in the US, to save the fast declining breed. In 1992 the breed was renamed Chantilly, as there was now a different breed in the UK by the name of Tiffanie.

Description: The Chantilly is a medium sized cat of foreign build. The head is medium sized with a short, broad muzzle which is fairly square in appearance and there is a slight nose break. The coat is semi-long, very silky, with a plumed tail and full ruff on the chest. The ears are medium sized with rounded tips, the eyes oval.

Colors: The Chantilly is always Chocolate in color, which is rich and full. The eyes are gold or amber.

Temperament: The Chantilly is neither placid nor energetic, it has rather found a comfortable niche in between the two extremes. A loyal cat which often attaches itself firmly to one particular person, the Chantilly is friendly and tolerates handling by children. The Chantilly loves company and does not like to be left on its own for long periods of time. It is a talkative cat, but nowhere near as vocal as the Oriental breeds.

Chartreux

AACE, ACA, ACFA, CFA, CFF, TICA, CA

Origin: The Chartreux originated in France, and stories of this breed have been told since the 16th century. It is believed that the Chartreux is a descendant of a breed known as "the cat of Syria," which had arrived in Europe during the crusades. The name Chartreux was first used during the 17th century when the breed became known as "the cat of France," and was said to be much prized both for its pelt and meat! The Chartreux existed in wild colonies in France, although these were small in numbers and it was not until after World War I that French cat breeders decided to preserve this breed, and started breeding it purposefully. These days, there are no Chartreux living wild, but the breed looks the same as it always has done.

Description: The Chartreux is a large cat, with a very dense, short coat, which should be water repellent. The head is very broad, although it lacks the short face of the Exotic or Persian. The ears are of medium size set high on the head, the eyes round. The body is medium in length and very robust with broad shoulders and a deep chest while The legs are comparatively short.

Colors: The Chartreux comes in one color only: Blue. This can be any shade of blue from ash grey to slate blue, and the tips of each hair are lightly ticked with a silver color. The eyes are copper, gold, or orange in color.

Temperament: The Chartreux is a calm and laid back cat, with a friendly disposition. They are said to avoid conflict, walking away from a confrontation rather than staying to fight.

The breed has good hunting skills, and therefore loves to play with toys like balls and toy mice. The Chartreux is very devoted to its owner, yet they are not overly attention seeking, and do not mind being alone at times. It is a very quiet breed of cat, seldom using its low pitched voice.

Colorpoint Shorthair

CFA

Origin: The Colorpoint Shorthair is the CFA's name for a Siamese that is not of any of the traditional Siamese colors. Originally, the Siamese came in four colors; Seal Point, Blue Point, Chocolate Point, and Lilac Point. To introduce the red series into the breed, outcrosses to other breeds such as the Abyssinian were made, and as such, some breeders did not consider this cat to be a pure-bred Siamese. In 1964, the CFA recognized the breed as Colorpoint Shorthair.

Description: The Colorpoint Shorthair should be exactly the same as the Siamese; a medium sized cat with a very slender, long body. The head is long and wedge shaped with tall, pointed ears. The eyes are almond shaped and a vivid blue. The legs are long and slender, the tail long and whip-like. The coat is very short and close laying. The body is pale, although it often gets darker shading as the cat grows older, and has darker points on face, ears, legs, and tail.

Colors: Flame Point, Cream Point, Seal Lynx Point (with barring on legs and tail, and stripes with the characteristic "M" marking on the forehead), Chocolate Lynx Point, Blue Lynx Point, Lilac Lynx Point, Flame Lynx Point, Cream Lynx Point, Seal Tortie Point, Chocolate Tortie Point, Blue-Cream Point, Lilac-Cream Point, Seal Tortie Lynx Point, Chocolate Tortie Lynx Point, and Lilac-Cream Lynx Point.

Temperament: The Colorpoint Shorthair is just like any Siamese. It is an extremely intelligent breed and there is very little a cat of this type cannot work out how to do, in no time at all they will learn how to open doors, cupboards, and even the fridge (to steal food, of course). Colorpoint Shorthairs, like Siamese, seem to think on a different level to other cats and they find it easier to get on with like-minded cats, rather than with breeds that are their total opposite. The Colorpoint Shorthair is a very energetic cat, playful even in its old age. They love climbing and jumping, will sleep on top of the tallest cupboard, think nothing of climbing the curtains, and although they are very devoted to their owner (usually one person in the family) and like to be comfortably asleep on this person's lap, they are active for most of the day, always looking for adventures. They love warmth, possibly because of their slim bodies and short coat, and always seek out heat sources such as fires and radiators. A Colorpoint Shorthair will happily make friends with the family dog, and thinks nothing of snuggling up to a big dog if it is for the cat's convenience — dogs can be warm and cozy! The most obvious feature of Colorpoint Shorthair behavior is probably their voice. Like Siamese they are very vocal cats, they will talk, they will answer back when spoken to, and they do so in a very loud voice — there is nothing quiet about a Colorpoint Shorthair. As such, this is an extraordinary cat which will make a perfect pet for those that like this specific temperament in cats; it is not a breed for those who like a quiet life with a cat serenely asleep all day.

Cornish Rex

AACE, ACA, AFC, CA, CFF, TICA, GCCF, CA

Origin: The Cornish Rex was the first of the different Rex breeds to appear, and it came about as a spontaneous mutation in an ordinary litter of non-pedigree kittens. The very first Rex cat was a male called "Kallibunker," born in 1950 in Cornwall, England. The owner of the litter of kittens, Mrs Ennismore, fortunately realized that she had a new mutation on her hands, and so set about contacting various people within the cat fancy in order to get a breeding program underway. Many people were involved in the development of this new breed, with its soft, short, and entirely curly fur. As the development of the breed required a fair amount of inbreeding to "Kallibunker's" relatives, to fix the gene responsible for the curly coat, the cats involved eventually became small and started to suffer from fertility problems. In due course outcrosses to other cats were needed, and so the breed gained in both strength and numbers. By the 1960s the Cornish Rex had become a popular show cat, and the breed had spread to many other countries worldwide. Other Rex mutations had also been discovered; similar coat types but different genes. When mated together, two Rex cats of different genes would produce only normal coated kittens.

comfortable lap to sit on. They often choose one human as their favorite person and this person they will treat like another cat, right down to washing and grooming! The Cornish Rex is curious and mischievous, likes to know what's going on, and is always alert when awake. They are highly intelligent cats which easily learn tricks such as opening doors. They love climbing and jumping, and this is not a breed for those that prefer a quiet cat which spends most of its time asleep.

Description: The Cornish Rex is a lot less exaggerated than its cousin, the Devon Rex. It is of medium size, with a medium length head and fairly tall ears, yet not as long and slender as the Siamese or Oriental. It is a very muscular cat and the legs are long, the tail long and fine. The coat is, of course, the most distinguishing feature of the breed. This is short and plush, very soft, and it lacks the longer, coarser guard hairs found in normal-coated cats. The entire coat is curly, but particularly so on the back of the cat. Even the whiskers and the eyebrows are wavy. Kittens often show bald patches, but this is considered a fault in an adult Cornish Rex. Occasionally, young adult Cornish Rexes do show bald patches, but grow fur by the time the cat has reached 18-24 months of age.

Colors: All colors and patterns are accepted in the Cornish Rex.

Temperament: Cornish Rexes are people cats, they adore companionship, and like nothing more than a

Cymric

AACE, ACA, ACFA, TICA, CA

Origin: The Cymric originated in the US during the 1960s, and is the long-haired version of the Manx. It is not recognized by the GCCF as the Manx is part of the British Shorthair group and logically a British Shorthair could not be longhaired. The CFA and CFF consider the Cymric to be a long-haired Manx, and simply recognize the breed as such.

Quite how the Manx could develop long fur is not entirely known; possibly it was a spontaneous mutation as has happened in so many other breeds, or breeders may at times have crossed Persian into the British Shorthair lines to improve type. It is, however, believed that the original Manx cats on the Isle of Man came in both Shorthair and Longhair.

Description: The Cymric is a semi-longhaired cat entirely without a tail. As with the Manx, kittens with short tails, known as "stumpies," and also kittens with full tails, "longies," are often born. The latter are used for breeding but not showing as it is

advisable not to mate two entirely tailless Cymrics together (referred to as "rumpies"), as this could cause deformities to occur in the kittens.

The Cymric is a robust and rounded cat. Of medium size, with a very short back. The hindlegs are longer than the frontlegs, and the Cymric therefore moves with an unusual gait, similar to that of a rabbit. The head is round with full cheeks, although the head of the UK Manx is often more rounded than in that seen in the US. The nose is long and without a break, while the ears are large with rounded tips, and the eyes large and round. The coat must be very dense, water resistant, and have a silky texture. It is at its fullest on the chest, and falls fairly flat on the body.

Colors: Any color or pattern apart from the pointed Himalayan pattern is acceptable in the Cymric.

Temperament: The Cymric is a friendly and outgoing cat, a breed of cat totally without any exaggerations in temperament. Playful and curious, fearless and friendly, the Cymric is not overly energetic, yet neither is it totally laid back. The Cymric gets on well with other cats of any breed as well as dogs, and is usually very good with children. Its lack of a tail renders it less agile than any cat with a full tail, but the Cymric is not particularly hindered by this, and gets on with life much in the same way as any other cat would.

Devon Rex

AACE, ACA, ACFA, CFA, CFF, GCCF, CA

Origin: The Devon Rex was the second type of Rex cat to appear, and like the first, the Cornish Rex, it came about as a spontaneous mutation. The first Cornish Rex kitten had been born in 1950, and ten years later in 1960, a Rex kitten was featured in the *Daily Mirror* newspaper which incorrectly stated that this was the only Rex-coated kitten in the UK. This kitten was the great grandson of the original Rex. Upon seeing this article, a Miss Beryl Cox from Devon contacted the breeder of the featured kitten, saying that she, too, owned a curly-coated kitten. She had looked after this kitten for some time, and his parentage was unknown. The kitten's name was "Kirlee," and his looks were different to that of the Cornish Rex, with a more exaggerated type. It was originally believed that "Kirlee" was of the same mutation as the Cornish Rex, but when mated to Cornish Rex queens, all the kittens were born with a normal coat, thus proving that "Kirlee" was indeed of a different mutated gene. This mutation eventually became recognized as the Devon Rex.

Description: The Devon Rex is the most distinctive of the Rex breeds, with its large ears and pixie-like face. Whereas the Cornish Rex has a slender but fairly ordinary body, the Devon Rex stands out from the crowd, with its oversized ears and short, wedge shaped head. The cheeks are very full, giving a broad head. The Devon Rex is a medium sized cat, with a slender but heavy and muscular body. The tail is long and slender, the legs slim and the paws small. The coat

is curled or waved all over the body, with kittens often showing a large degree of baldness; the coat will regrow as the kitten grows older. The whiskers and the eyebrows are shorter than in normal coated cats, and these too are curly.

Colors: All coat colors and markings are acceptable in the Devon Rex.

Temperament: The Devon Rex is a very affectionate cat, the sort of cat that will crave human company. Sit down on a chair, and the Devon Rex will immediately be on your lap. Walk around the house, and the Devon Rex will follow. The Devon Rex is a very forward and outgoing cat, always looking out for new adventures, always ready to play whatever game is on offer, always curious to see what is going on. It is an extremely intelligent and energetic breed, which either is on the go at full speed, or fast asleep. The Devon Rex gets on well with everyone, be it other cats (of whatever breed), dogs, other pets, adults, or children. They will tolerate handling by children without lashing out, and they are very good at making themselves comfortable, thinking nothing of snuggling up in the fur on top of a sleeping dog's back, if that happens to be the most comfortable and warm spot available. They crave warmth, and kittens with little fur will feel like a hot water bottle to the touch, as the body temperature is slightly raised to compensate for the lack. The Devon Rex is not a particularly vocal cat, but it is very much a cat for those who want a lively and playful pet, and a lonely Devon would be a very unhappy cat — it will need either constant human or feline company.

Egyptian Mau

AACE, ACA, ACFA, CFA, CFF, TICA, CA

Origin: Anther old and natural breed, like the Abyssinian, the history of the Egyptian Mau is unclear. Believed to have developed in Egypt, the first documented Egyptian Maus were owned by the Princess Nathalie Troubetskoy, a Polish born Russian who first emigrated to England, then served as a nurse for the American army in Italy, before settling in America. While living in Rome, the Princess was given an Egyptian Mau kitten by a friend. The kitten, named "Baba," may not have been the first Mau owned by the Princess, but records are unclear. In 1956, the Princess left Italy for the US, and then brought with her three Egyptian Maus, which became the foundation stock in her breeding program. As three cats were such a limited gene pool, out-crosses to domestic cats (i.e. moggies) were probably done. The breed was first recognized in 1968 by the Canadian Cat Association, later to be followed by US registries.

Description: The Egyptian Mau is a Spotted Tabby shorthair, with a body that is not as rounded as that of the American Shorthair, yet not as svelte as that of the Oriental. The ears are large, and the face of medium-length. The cat should be fairly large, although the females can, naturally, be quite a bit smaller than the males once they have reached maturity. The coat is short and lays flat, and it should be dense. The legs are long, with the hind legs being slightly longer than the front legs. The toes on the hind paws should be longer than those on the front paws.

Colors: Always Spotted, with green or amber eyes. The entire body should be spotted, ideally with round, even spots, of equal size. The legs and tail are barred, and the face shows the classical "M" tabby marking on the forehead. Various colors exist; like Bronze, Silver, and Smoke, with the spots being black or blue of different shades, depending upon the body color.

Temperament: The Egyptian Mau is a sensitive breed, which in its early beginnings could be rather bad tempered, no doubt due to its wild ancestors. These days, it is a lively, intelligent, and active cat, and as breeders have worked hard to perfect the temperament, the cats are now friendly, attentive, and quite vocal, though preferring to talk in a much smaller voice than that of Oriental cats.

European Shorthair

CA

Origin: As the US has its American Shorthair, and the UK the British Shorthair; the European Shorthair is the native breed of Sweden. Little known outside the Scandinavian countries, the European Shorthair is the pedigree version of the ordinary moggy. In 1946, the first native Swedish shorthaired cats were registered, and this was originally under the name of Swedish Housecat. This name was later changed to European Shorthair, as this seemed a more suitable description. The breed never became very popular, and in the early days it was judged along the lines of the breed standard for the British Shorthair, which is a cat of entirely different type. It was not until 1981 that the two breeds were given separate recognition by the FIFe, which is the international body that the CA is affiliated to.

Description: At a first glance, the European Shorthair may look like any domestic cat or moggy. On closer inspection though, it is not difficult to see that this cat has been refined so that its color is richer than that of non-pedigree cats, and the type does not vary as it would in randomly bred cats. The European Shorthair is a medium sized cat, with a rectangular body which should show substantial bone structure and be well muscled. The neck is of a good length and muscular. The legs are of average length, and these too are muscular and powerful. The head looks fairly large in comparison to the body; it is slightly longer than it is wide, but when viewed from the front it does appear to be rounded and there is a slight nose break between the eyes. The nose is of medium length, straight and broad. The cheeks are well developed. The ears are medium sized with rounded tips, the eyes large and round. The coat is always short, and this should be dense and glossy, and show resistance to water.

Colors: Most colors are accepted, but not those of the Chocolate and Lilac series, the Cinnamon and Fawn series, or pointed Himalayan-pattern cats.

Temperament: A European Shorthair is a happy medium of a cat; there are no exaggerations either in body or behavior. A friendly, playful, and highly intelligent cat with a good nature, the European Shorthair is curious and happy to take part in games, yet it is not too energetic and will be just as happy to sit down for a cuddle with its owner as it will be to play with toys or other cats.

Exotic Longhair

AACE, ACA, ACFA, CFF

Origin: The Exotic Longhair is not, as such, a breed in its own right. It is a by-product of Exotic Shorthair breeding. As the Exotic was originally bred from crosses between the Persian and the American Shorthair (US) and the Persian and the British Shorthair (UK), it followed that most Exotic Shorthairs would carry the gene for longhair. In the US today, the Exotic is becoming increasingly common, and homozygous Exotics are to be found; that is, Exotics that have been bred from Shorthair to Shorthair matings for generations, and which do not any longer carry the recessive Longhair gene. However, it is fair to say that most Exotic Shorthairs worldwide do carry the Longhair gene, and thus it is inevitable that in most litters of Exotics, the odd Longhair kitten will be born. How these longhaired kittens are treated, depends on the registry in which they are registered. The AACE, ACFA, ACA, and CFF consider them to be Longhair Exotic, a separate breed. Some registries consider them to be Persian, and these cats can be shown alongside other Persians, and can also be used in Persian breeding programs. Others, such as the GCCF, see the longhaired Exotic as simply a by-product, termed a Variant, which cannot be shown, nor used for breeding with breeds other than the Exotic.

Description: The Exotic Longhair looks exactly like a Persian. There is no way that anybody can tell that the cat is Longhaired Exotic and not a purebred Persian just by looking at it. The two breeds are identical in looks, and the Exotic Longhair can have just as full a coat as a Persian. It will have other breeds in its genetic make-up, but will not be able to produce short-hair kittens if mated to longhaired cats.

Colors: All the colors and patterns that the Exotic and Persian comes in.

Temperament: The Exotic Longhair may look like a Persian, but is slightly more outgoing and adventurous than the average Persian. The Longhair Exotic is a friendly lap cat which loves company, yet it will have a lot of playfulness too. It is a curious cat that likes to know what is going on, and it gets on well with most other cats and dogs.

Exotic Shorthair

AACE, ACA, ACFA, CFA, CFF, TICA, GCCF, CA

Origin: The Exotic originally developed as a by-product of other pedigree cat breeding. Breeders in the US had introduced Persians into their breeding programs of American Shorthairs, to improve the type of their cats. It was found that the resulting first cross kittens were very different to any other type of cat; they showed the type of the Persian with its flat, rounded face and cobby body, yet had a short coat unlike any other cat. The coat was so dense that it stood out from the body and did not lay flat. Consequently, some breeders decided to continue breeding from these cats, and the Exotic Shorthair was created; the shorthaired version of the Persian. The breed was first granted recognition in the US in 1967. In the UK, development was slower, but continued in a similar way. Whereas the American Exotics had been the by-products of American Shorthairs mated to Persians, in the UK it was breeders of British Shorthairs that mated their cats to Persians, and the resulting kittens were very similar to those seen in the US. Thus the Exotic Shorthair in the US has American Shorthair and

Persian as its ancestors (and at some time, Burmese were crossed in, too), but the UK Exotic is derived from British Shorthair and Persian. In the UK, the breed did not get preliminary recognition until 1986, with full championship status as late as 1995. The popularity of the Exotic is now growing worldwide, as it is such an ideal cat for those who like the Persian look, yet cannot spare the time for the extensive grooming involved.

Description: The Exotic has earned many descriptions, "the shorthaired Persian," "the lazy man's Persian," "the Persian in a mini-skirt," and also "the Teddy bear cat." The Exotic is to all intents and purposes a shorthaired Persian. Its body is medium to large in size, cobby and heavy, with short, sturdy legs, a short tail with a nicely rounded tip, a round head with a completely flat profile, small, rounded ears spaced well apart, and large, round eyes. The coat is very important; this is dense and short, yet not as short as in most other Shorthair breeds, and it must not lay flat. In a really good

example, the coat is so dense that it will stand out from the body.

Colors: The Exotic is recognized in all colors and markings found in the Persian cat, which is most colors that exist in pedigree cats. Popular varieties include Selfs in Blue, Black, White, and Cream, Tabbies (in particular Brown and Red), Colorpointed and Bicolor, but many other color varieties exist.

Temperament: The Exotic is an excellent pet cat. Placid and friendly with an excellent nature, it is more outgoing than the Persian, loves games, is very curious, and likes to know what is going on. The breed, perhaps due to its mixed ancestry, tend to get along with any other type of cat, as well as dogs and other pets. The Exotic temperament really shows the best of both worlds; a friendly lap cat that enjoys human companionship, yet an independent cat that retains its playfulness throughout its life. The Exotic is not particularly vocal, and makes an excellent pet for most people.

German Rex

CA

Origin: Like all the other Rex breeds, the German Rex appeared as a spontaneous mutation; a curly coated kitten born into a litter of ordinary moggy kittens in Germany. It is not a widely recognized breed; interest in this mutation has been relatively low, due to its many similarities to the Cornish Rex.

Description: The German Rex is very similar in appearance to the Cornish Rex. The cat's body is of medium size and length, and it should be well muscled, yet not fat. The cat should feel heavier than it looks; there is substance to the body, which is slender, yet not overly Oriental-like. The legs are also fairly slender and of average length. The tail is medium in length, tapering to a rounded tip. The head is medium long and slightly rounded with well developed cheeks. Ears are of medium size as are the eyes which should be slightly slanted. The obvious feature of the German Rex is its coat. This is very soft and should feel like velvet to the touch. The coat is short and either waved or curled all over the body, there must be no bald patches present, although German Rex kittens often go through a stage where they have the odd bare area on the body. This coat will grow as the cat gets older.

Colors: Any color or pattern can be seen in the German Rex.

Temperament: The German Rex is a very friendly and playful cat, yet not as energetic as the Oriental breeds. A faithful cat which will chose one person as its special friend, it will be happy to spend hours napping on that person's lap. Being a curious cat, the German Rex will be happy to follow its owner around the house to see what is going on, and it will take great delight in playing with toys such as balls or toy mice. A breed that likes to jump and climb, the German Rex is an agile cat, but not quite the same mischief maker as its distant cousin the Devon Rex. With its short fur, the German Rex craves warmth, and will happily sleep in front of a fire, or snuggled up to another cat during the colder months. Not a breed that likes to be without company, the German Rex is happiest with other, like-minded, cats.

Havana (Brown)

AACA, ACA, ACFA, CA, CFA, CFF, TICA, GCCF

Origin: The Havana is part of the Oriental group; some registries refer to it as the Havana Brown, others as the Oriental Havana.

The Oriental derives from the Siamese. Siamese cats that had, by accident, been crossed with non-pedigree Shorthairs, started to produce Siamese-shaped kittens of colors other than the usual, pointed Siamese colors. One such kitten was bred in 1952, by Siamese breeder Isobel Monro Smith in the UK. The kitten was all brown; a Havana. Several other breeders got interested in the idea of creating a new breed just like the Siamese but of other colors. Today, the Oriental Shorthair comes in a large number of different colors, of which the Havana is one of the most popular. Its body shape is exactly the same as that of the Siamese.

Description: The Havana is a Siamese in all but color; it has a medium sized, long, and slender body which is very elegant. The legs are long and slender, with the hind legs being slightly longer than the front legs. The head is wedge-shaped with large ears, and almond shaped eyes which are slightly slanted. The tail is long and whip like, tapering to a point. The coat is short and sleek, with a glossy shine.

Colors: The Havana should be a rich warm chestnut brown, with vividly green eyes.

Temperament: The Havana has the same temperament as all the other Oriental and Siamese breeds; an energetic extrovert of a cat which is very vocal. Highly intelligent, the Havana easily gets bored on its own, and wants companionship, both in the form of a favorite human as well as other cats of the same or similar breeds. The Havana likes to get involved in whatever goes in the household, and loves nothing more than getting into mischief. They are cats that love to jump and climb, and can often be found perching on top of the tallest cupboard or shelf.

Himalayan

AACE, ACFA, CFF, TICA
(Recognized as a Persian variety by the CFA, ACA, and GCCF)

Origin: This breed was developed independently in the US and the UK at virtually the same time. It was, however, first recognized in the UK in 1955 as the Colourpoint Persian, while in the US, it was first recognized, in 1957, as the Himalayan. It is still known as the Colourpoint Persian in most countries other than the US.

The creation of the Colourpoint in Britain came about as a pure fluke. The man behind the creation of this new breed was Brian Stirling-Webb, a noted Siamese breeder. It has been documented that Mr Stirling-Webb had absolutely no wish to create a longhaired version of the Siamese, yet at a Siamese show in 1947, he was approached by a woman who claimed to own a longhaired Siamese, and asked if Stirling-Webb would allow one of his Siamese stud cats to mate this queen. Mr Stirling-Webb opposed this mating, and correctly pointed out that any such mating would, in any event, only produce shorthair kittens, as the shorthair gene is a dominant one. Instead, he suggested that the queen's owner had her cat mated to a Persian, if she indeed was to breed from her at all. The queen's owner was not happy with either of Mr Stirling-Webb's suggestions, and asked if she could at least bring her cat for him to have a look at.

When Stirling-Webb eventually got to see this supposedly longhaired Siamese, named "Bubastis Georgina," he was taken aback by the beauty of the cat. Far from being a slender, Siamese type cat, this queen had almost Persian features but with the traditional seal point Siamese coloring. Amazingly, nothing was known about how this cat had developed, as she was a former stray which had been living in a church yard before being adopted by her owner.

This queen inspired Stirling-Webb to create a Siamese colored Persian cat. At first, he mated Seal Point and Blue Point Siamese to Black and Blue Persians, then crossed the kittens together. Eventually he had founded a strain of longhaired, pointed cats with Persian body shape.

Meanwhile, US breeders had worked equally hard to create the same breed, but by using slightly different methods. In the US, the first matings were between Siamese and Silver and Smoke colored Persians. These colors were less suitable for pointed breeding than self Blue and/or Black, so this may be the reason for why the breed took longer to gain recognition in the US.

For many years, the Himalayan was the poor relative of the Persian, with few cats being of the same facial and body type as other Persians, but these days, there is nothing to distinguish the Himalayan from other Persians as regards type.

Description: The Himalayan is a medium to large sized cat, with short, stocky legs, a short tail, small, rounded ears set well apart, and a round face with a perfectly flat profile. The eyes are large and round and spaced well apart. The cat is heavy and the coat should cover the entire body; with a full tail, and a large ruff that frames the cat's face. The fuller the coat on the body, the better. The bite must be level; an undershot bite is a fault which is often seen in Persians.

Colors: There are 20 recognized colors of the Himalayan. The body should always be as pale as possible, any darker shading is considered a fault, in particular on the back and tummy. The eyes are always blue and the face mask, ears, legs, and tail are colored. The basic colors are Seal (a dark brown, which is what the self Black becomes when combined with the pointed gene), Blue, Chocolate, Lilac, Flame (Red in the UK), Cream, Tortie, Blue Tortie (Blue-Cream in the UK), Chocolate Tortie, Lilac Tortie (Lilac-Cream), and then the same ten colors in Lynx Point (Tabby Point in the UK); the points are broken up by tabby stripes, with striped legs, a ringed tail, and tabby markings with the classic "M" feature on the face.

Temperament: The Himalayan is in many ways the ideal pet cat; at least for those that fully understand that its coat needs very regular grooming to not become severely matted (the consequences of this would be that the cat would have to be shaved). The Himalayan is a placid and gentle cat; a lap cat that greatly enjoys its owner's company and is cuddly and friendly with a great tolerance level. The Himalayan gets on with most other animals, in particular other cats and dogs. It loves a quiet life, enjoys comforts such as a nice, comfortable spot to sleep in and a warm fire in the winter. Yet this is a playful and curious cat which thinks nothing of getting shut inside cupboards when the desire to explore becomes too much. The Himalayan will retain most of its kitten characteristics during its life, and it is not as docile as other Persians. It also talks, not as loudly as a Siamese but in a quiet, demanding voice, asking for attention and food. This is probably due to its past Siamese connection.

Japanese Bobtail

AACE, ACA, ACFA, CFA, CFF, TICA, CA

Origin: The Japanese Bobtail cat does, of course, originate from Japan. This is a naturally occuring ancient breed, which, from written records, is believed to have existed thousands of years ago and first arrived in Japan from either China or Korea. The first Japanese Bobtails were imported to the US from Japan in 1968, by cat fancier Elizabeth Freret, and the breed was recognized by the CFA in 1971. The Japanese Bobtail is not seen in the UK.

Description: The Japanese Bobtail is a medium sized cat, well muscled but slender rather than heavy in build. The face is long with high cheekbones and forms an equilateral triangle. The ears are large and set well apart and the eyes are large and oval, set wide apart and slightly slanted. The body is long, and there must be no tendency towards cobbiness. The legs are long and slender, with the hindlegs noticeably longer than the frontlegs. The coat can be either short or semi-long, and in the longhair the coat lays flat. The tail is the prominent feature of the Japanese Bobtail, it is short and should resemble a rabbit's tail, with the hair fanning out from it, camouflaging the

bone. The tail is actually unique to each cat, as its structure can vary a lot. It should be no longer than three inches, and it may be curved, angled, kinked, flexible, or rigid.

Colors: White, Black, Red, Black and White, Red and White, Mi-Ke (tricolor), Tortoiseshell. These are the most commonly seen colors in the Japanese Bobtail. Other colors do occur, but Chocolate, Lavender, Pointed (such as in Siamese) or unpatterned agouti colors (such as in the Abyssinian) are not allowed.

Temperament: The Japanese Bobatil is an intelligent cat, which is active and playful. Kittens mature quickly and adults remain playful for all of their lives. The Japanese Bobtail is a very friendly cat which loves human company, and so does not like to be left on its own. They enjoy playing with toys such as balls or toy mice and are keen on jumping and climbing. They get on well with other cats and dogs and are very tolerant of children. The Japanese Bobtail is a talkative breed that likes to have conversations with its owner.

Javanese

CFA, CA

Origin: The Javanese is simply a Balinese cat of colors other than the original four Siamese/Balinese colors; Seal Point, Blue Point, Chocolate Point, and Lilac Point. The name Javanese is taken from the name of the island next to Bali; Java.

As outcrosses to other breeds were necessary to create the red series colors in the Siamese, some breeders did not accept these cats as true Siamese, and the CFA instead registered them as Colorpoint Shorthair. Thus the longhaired version of the Colorpoint Shorthair is the Javanese. Just like the Balinese had originated through long-

haired kittens occasionally turning up in Siamese litters, the Javanese originated from longhaired kittens born to Colorpoint Shorthairs.

Description: The Javanese is a true Siamese/Colorpoint Shorthair in all but coat, which is semi-long. On the body, the coat lays flat, with a larger ruff on the chest which tends to be fuller during colder weather. The tail is the most striking feature of the Javanese, as there the coat is at its fullest. In every other respect, the Javanese has the same looks as the Colorpoint Shorthair, with the long,

svelte and elegantly slender body, a long wedge shaped face, tall, pricked ears, long slender legs, and vividly blue eyes. The cat is of medium size.

Colors: This breed comes in the same colors as the Colorpoint Shorthair: Flame Point, Cream Point, Seal Lynx Point (with barring on legs and tail, and stripes with the characteristic "M" marking on the forehead), Chocolate Lynx Point, Blue Lynx Point, Lilac Lynx Point, Flame Lynx Point, Cream Lynx Point, Seal Tortie Point, Chocolate Tortie Point, Blue-Cream Point, Lilac-Cream Point, Seal Tortie Lynx Point, Chocolate Tortie Lynx Point, and Lilac-Cream Lynx Point.

Temperament: The Javanese is an extrovert, just like the Balinese. It is extremely intelligent, energetic, lively, playful, and loves jumping and climbing. It will easily learn how to open doors, and will like nothing more than getting up to mischief. The Javanese is a very single minded cat, dominant in temperament, which will go through with whatever he or she has decided to do; there is no stopping a determined Javanese! A very vocal cat, the Javanese will talk to you, answer back every time it is spoken to, and if it does not get its own way or wants an early dinner, it will yell at its owner in a very loud voice indeed. Javanese cats tend to be very devoted to their particular owner, but may find it hard to accept strangers. They do not like to be left on their own and are happier being kept in the company of other cats, particularly cats of the same or a similar breed, as at times the Javanese may find it difficult to get on with cats of breeds that are markedly different to its own temperament.

Kashmir

CFF

Origin: The Kashmir is not really a separate breed; it is a Colorpoint Carrier (known as CPC). When a Himalayan/Colorpoint Persian is mated to a Persian of any other color than another pointed cat, the kittens will not be pointed, but will instead carry the pointed gene. If the Colorpoint Carriers then in turn are mated to pointed cats (or other carriers of the gene) they can produce pointed kittens. Most registries will recognize the Colorpoint Carrier cats as simply any other Persian as they will look the same. However, the CFF chooses to register these cats as Kashmir cats. The reasoning behind this is that as the Himalayan/Colorpoint Persian was originally bred from crosses between Siamese and Persians, it is not a pure-bred Persian. However, as there has been a lapse of nearly 50 years since any Siamese blood were introduced into the breed, most registries consider the cats to be purebred Persians.

Description: The Kashmir will be a Persian cat with all the usual Persian characteristics; a medium to large body, which is short, compact, and cobby, short sturdy legs, a broad, round head with a very flat profile, small rounded ears spaced well apart, and large, round eyes, together with a full coat. The only differ-

ence between the Kashmir and other Persians of the same color is that the Kasmir, carrying the pointed gene (which leads to blue eyes), often has a poor, rather diluted, eye color. In other words, a Kashmir of a color that is meant to have bright orange or copper eyes, may instead show pale yellow or amber eyes.

Colors: Any color except for the pointed Himalayan pattern.

Temperament: The Kashmir will be a true Persian in temperament. It is a laid back and placid cat which is very friendly. The Kashmir likes to snuggle up on its owner's lap, does not mind being left on its own for a while but prefers to have another feline companion. Not the most active or intelligent of cats, the Kashmir is nonetheless curious and playful.

Korat

AACE, ACA, ACFA, CFA, CFF, TICA, GCCF, CA

Origin: The Korat is in ancient breed that originated in Thailand, alongside the Siamese and the Burmese. This cat was seen as a symbol of good luck; the silver colored tips to its coat were said to signify wealth, and its blue coat and green eyes meant rich harvests and good fertility. The Thai name of the breed is "Si-sawat," which means grayish blue. It is believed that Korat cats were exhibited at the very first cat show at London's Crystal Palace in 1871, although these were described as "Blue Siamese" and there is no proof that these cats were, in fact, Korats. What is known, is that the breed officially reached the US in 1959, and the UK in 1972.

Description: Since the Korat's arrival in the cat fancy, its type, characteristics, and temperament has been preserved and there has always been a policy of no outcrossing to other breeds. All the Korats of today can be traced right back to the original Thai imports, and the Korat breeders take great pride in the fact that the breed is an ancient and totally natural breed. The Korat is still required to look just the same as the Korat cat described in a poem written centuries ago: "The base of each hair, is the color of a cloud," and the Korat's distinctive eyes are "Like dew when dropped on the leaf of the lotus."

Another of the Korat's most distinguishing features is its head, which is heart shaped. The eyes, as indicated above, are particularly large and a luminous green. The Korat is a medium sized cat, yet heavy, the females should be smaller and daintier than the males. The coat is short and should lay close to the body. This is the most breathtaking feature of the Korat and is blue with generous silver tipping, giving it a silver sheen.

Colors: It has been said that if a Korat is not silver blue, then it is not a Korat. Yet despite the fact that no outcrosses to other breeds have been made, two color variations have been carried recessively in the breed. Thus, different colored kittens are occasionally born in Korat litters. At present these colors are only acknowledged in the UK although there are records of them being born in other countries too. The two variations are known as the Thai Bluepoint, which is a cat very similar to the old, chunkier style, Siamese, and the Thai Lilac, with a solid Lilac coat, showing some of the silver tipping.

Temperament: Korats are faithful companions that like company and do not like being on their own. They are intelligent, lively, and playful, and so demand a fair amount of interaction from their owners. The Korat is a cat that loves to play, particularly retrieving small toys. They are talkative and exhibit a wide range of different sounds, yet they are not as vocal as the Siamese.

LaPerm

ACFA

Origin: The LaPerm was not a deliberately created breed; it first developed as a spontaneous mutation. The very first LaPerm kitten was born in a litter of ordinary moggy kittens belonging to cherry farmers Linda and Richard Koehl from Dallas. Their tabby cat, "Speedy," which had been acquired along with several others simply to help rid the farm of mice and other pests, gave birth to a litter of six kittens in 1982. Five of these kittens looked like ordinary moggies, but the sixth was different. The kitten was completely bald, and had a much longer face than its siblings and mother. It also had much bigger ears. After a few weeks, fur started to grow on the

kitten's pink little body, and this turned out to be both unusually soft and curly. Indeed, the kitten was named "Curly," and kept by the Koehls. She soon proved to have a different temperament to her siblings, being much more affectionate. Further litters were born to the farm cats and more kittens like "Curly" started to appear, sometimes several per litter. These litters were bred from "Curly's" mother and her descendants and the curly coat appeared in both shorthairs and longhairs. For years, the Koehls made no attempt to deliberately breed these curly coated cats, but their numbers grew naturally, and visitors to the farm started asking questions about this apparently new breed of cat. The Koelhs then started controlled breeding, and decided to call their new breed LaPerm.

Description: The LaPerm can have either a short or long coat, but this is always very soft and very curly. These days, kittens are not usually born without any fur, but instead with a straight coat, which starts to curl after a few weeks. The LaPerm does indeed look a cat that has had a perm done at the hairdresser! The body is slightly Foreign in build, being sleek with a long face and tall ears, but it is not as exaggerated as the body of a Siamese or Oriental. The size is small to medium.

Colors: Any color or combination of colors are allowed.

Temperament: The LaPerm is a people loving cat, a breed which thrives on attention, happily spends hours on its owner's lap, and which prefers to stay indoors with human company rather than explore the great outdoors. This makes them suitable for people who live in apartment buildings. They are openly affectionate and are often said to enjoy kissing their owners. The coat needs minimal grooming and does not tend to mat in the longhairs.

Maine Coon

AACE, ACA, ACFA, CFA, CFF, TICA, GCCF, CA

Origin: Many legends have surrounded the Maine Coon breed. It has been said the cat came about as a cross between domestic cats and the American lynx, or even between a cat and a racoon. These days, the most common misconception about the breed is its size. The Maine Coon is a very large breed of cat, with some males reaching a weight of 25 pounds, but rumors tell of cats much bigger.

The true origins of the Maine Coon are somewhat unclear, but it is believed that the breed developed in a similar way to the Norwegian Forest Cat. Indeed, the two breeds may have originated from the same stock of cats, brought to Maine by the Vikings. The Maine Coon is a very old and entirely natural breed with a long and weather proof coat which developed to enable it to survive in rough and varying climates. It has been known in the US since the very start of the cat fancy, but the Maine Coon only entered the UK in the early 1980s.

Description: The Maine Coon is a large semi-longhair cat, which is described to be of "medium Foreign type." It is somewhat rectangular in appearance — a heavy and solidly built cat, which is muscular and powerful. The coat is full during the colder months, with a very large neck ruff and a heavy, water resistant coat on

the body, together with a well plumed tail. During the warmer months the Maine Coon loses most of its long coat and can almost look shorthaired, with just a slightly fluffy tail. The head is of medium length and square looking, and the profile shows no break or stop. The ears are large and pointed, with tufts on the tips, while the eyes are round and set well apart. The legs are in proportion to the body and are thickset. The neck is substantial, with many Maine Coons being far too wide around the neck for any collar intended for pet cats to fit them. The tail is long.

Colors: Any color or pattern is allowed, except for the pointed Himalayan pattern, Chocolate, or Lilac. The most popular color is, without doubt, the Brown Tabby, often combined with white, as this color gives the cat a very wild and natural look. Red, Silver, and Cream Tabbies are also popular, as are Tortoiseshells and Torbies in various combinations.

Temperament: The Maine Coon can perhaps be best described as a dog-like cat. Not only does it have the size of a small or even medium sized dog, but it is a cat that loves to follow its owner around, will happily play retrieving games, and does not get intimidated easily. Maine Coons from the best bloodlines are usually very friendly and outgoing cats which happily greet any stranger, but some Maine Coons do have a tendency to nervousness, something which prospective owners should bear in mind when choosing a kitten — look out for parents that are forthcoming and friendly, and the kittens are likely to be the same. The Maine Coon is not really a lap cat, preferring to be on the go, but it is not overly energetic either. It gets on well with cats of all other breeds as well as dogs.

Manx

AACE, ACA, ACFA, CFA, TICA, GCCF, CA

Origin: The Manx cat, from the Isle of Man in Britain, is a very old breed of cat. Manx cats were present at the first ever cat show, staged in 1871, in London, and around the same time, written records state that it was believed that the Manx cat originally came to the Isle of Man on Spanish vessels, part of the Spanish Armada in the 1500s. In the UK, the Manx is now part of the British Shorthair group.

Description: The obvious feature of the Manx is its lack of a tail. The show quality Manx has no tail at all, some-thing which is referred to as a "rumpy." Kittens with very short tails are also born, known as "stumpies." These are used for breeding, but not showing. As it is inadvisable to mate two rumpy Manx cats together, cats with full tails are used in the breeding programs; these are known as "longies."

The back of the Manx is very short, and the hind legs are considerably longer than the front legs. Thus the Manx cat moves rather like a rabbit. The Manx is a solid and compact cat of medium size. The head is large and

round with prominent cheeks, and the nose is broad but straight and the ears are quite large with rounded tips. The eyes are large and round and the breed possesses a dense coat, which should be water resistant.

Colors: Any color or pattern is acceptable, except for the pointed Siamese/Himalayan pattern.

Temperament: The Manx is a very average cat in temperament, a steady and straight forward sort of cat, which is neither lazy nor energetic. A playful cat when it feels like it, at other times the Manx will be at its happiest snuggled up in front of a warm fire, or on its owner's lap. The Manx gets on well with other cats and dogs. Being tailless, it has slightly less well developed balance than other cats, but a carefully bred Manx cat should show no actual handicaps. After all, the breed must be full of vigor as it survived for hundreds of years on the Isle of Man, without human interference.

Munchkin

ACFA, TICA

Origin: The Munchkin came about as a spontaneous mutation. This was only recently discovered by cat breeders within the fancy, but had been reported much earlier, even before World War I. This was in Germany in particular, where the cat was referred to as the "kangaroo cat." Eventually all of these short-legged cats seemed to disappear, but the mutation reappeared in the 1980s in Louisiana. Sandra Hochenedel from Rayville was looking to buy a pet cat for her children, when she found a pregnant cat living wild under a truck. She brought the cat home, named it "Blackberry," and only then realized that the cat's legs were much shorter than that of any ordinary cat. "Blackberry" went on to give birth to several litters, and each subsequent litter included both short-legged and long-legged kittens. Cat fanciers eventually got interested in the breed, which was named Munchkin after the short-legged people in *The Wizard of Oz*.

Description: The Munchkin looks like any ordinary cat, except for its short dwarf-like legs which are similar to the legs of a Dachshund, and are also slightly bowed. Unlike the Dachshund though, the Munchkin has been found to suffer from no spinal abnormalities and is said to be no more prone to skeletal problems than any ordinary long-legged cat. The Munchkin can be either shorthaired or longhaired. It is a medium sized breed, which naturally looks smaller than it actually is because of its short legs. The body is solid and rounded and must not be too slender nor too cobby. The head is the shape of an equilateral triangle, with medium sized ears and large walnut shaped eyes. The legs are only about half the size of ordinary cat's legs, with the elbows held higher; these should lie close to the cat's ribcage. The hind legs are slightly longer than the front legs. The semi-longhaired Munchkin has a weatherproof coat of a shaggy appearance.

Colors: Any color or pattern.

Temperament: The Munchkin is said to be the eternal kitten, a friendly and playful cat which never loses its kitten characteristics. Naturally, with such short legs, movement will be somewhat restricted compared to normal legged cats, especially jumping and climbing, but Munchkins are quite able to jump up onto chairs like any other cat. Some cat registries, like the GCCF, have, however, stated that they will not recognize a cat which shows this type of deformity.

Nebelung

CFF, TICA

Origin: The Nebelung is said to have been exhibited at the very first cat show, way back in 1871 at London's Crystal Palace. However, this breed, which, in essence, is a semi-longhair version of the Russian Blue, then apparently ceased to exist, and it was not until 1986 that the first modern day Nebelungs were registered in the US. The first two Nebelungs to be registered were a male, "Siegfried," and a female, "Brunhilde." Their first litter was born in 1986, and, shortly after, an application for new breed status was made to TICA. Nebelung is a German word which means "creature of the mist." The breed does indeed descend from the Russian Blue, and the two breed standards are very similar.

Description: The Nebelung is a small to medium sized cat, which should be of an elegant Foreign type. The body is long with fine bones, and the cat must not appear to be either heavy or chunky. The legs are long and slender, the paws small — the cat should appear to walk on tiptoes. The tail is long and the head is of medium length, with a straight nose without a break. The ears are large and set well apart. Eyes are almond shaped and slanted like in an Oriental. The coat is semi-long, and should be soft and shiny. The hairs are tipped with silver, and the coat reflects light, so giving the impression of the cat being surrounded by a light mist, hence the name. The coat is at its fullest on the tail which shows a fine plume.

Color: Medium Blue with silver tip-ping; the silver tips should be clearly seen if the coat is brushed backwards, as they will contrast with the darker undercolor. The eyes are a vivid green.

Temperament: The Nebelung is a fairly quiet and shy cat, a breed which does not greet strangers with enthusiasm, but which will be loving and loyal towards its own family. The Nebelung is a cat that likes to spend time on its owner's lap and they are curious cats that happily follow their owners around. A highly intelligent cat, the Nebelung will decide who it does or does not trust.

Norwegian Forest Cat

AACE, ACA, ACFA, CFA, CFF, TICA, GCCF, CA

Origin: The Norwegian Forest Cat is a natural breed, never purposefully developed but occuring naturally in its native Norway. Some folk tales tell of Norwegian Forest Cats being kept as early as the Viking age. One theory is that the Vikings brought home with them cats found during their journeys — semi-longhaired cats which were found living wild in countries such as France. These then interbred with the native cats of Norway. The exact origins of the breed will never be known, but it is a breed that existed and developed naturally for many years, without human intervention, like several other breeds. Pedigree breeders started capturing and breeding the semi-wild forest cats of Norway in the 1930s, but with advent of World War II, it was not until the early 1970s that the breed started to be properly kept and supervised by the cat fancy. These breeders had then come to realize that their native breed would face extinction unless a breeding program was worked out. There were fewer forest cats around, and those that were left needed to be used for further breeding with other forest cats, as opposed to allowing them to simply mate any farm cat that they happened to come across, as when the semi-longhaired forest cats mated shorthaired domestic cats, the offspring would invariably be shorthaired. The breed was eventually recognized in 1976 by the Federation Internationale Feline (FIFe), and its popularity spread to other countries, although it has always remained most popular in Scandinavia.

Description: The Norwegian Forest Cat is an entirely natural looking cat without any exaggerations. The cat is semi-longhaired with a large ruff on its chest in the winter, heavy feathering on the hind legs, and a long, bushy tail. During the warmer summer months, the cat's coat is much shorter. The ears are tall with tufts on the tips, the face moderately long. The Norwegian Forest Cat is a medium sized to large cat, powerful and muscular.

Colors: The Norwegian Forest Cat is recognized in all colors and patterns, except for Siamese pattern. The Tabbies are particularly popular; especially in Brown, Red, and Silver, with or without white markings. Black and white is also very commonly seen. Many breeders prefer these colors as they are the most natural looking, giving the impression of the cat indeed being wild.

Temperament: The Norwegian Forest Cat is an intelligent, fearless, and outgoing cat with an independent nature. Most Forest Cats will have one favorite person that they will become attached to, although they are not lap cats in the same sense as, for instance, Persians. They, and only they, will decide where and when they will grace their owner by settling on their lap. These cats get on well with cats of all other breeds as well as dogs.

104

Ocicat

AACE, ACA, ACFC, CFA, CFF, TICA, GCCF, CA

Origin: The Ocicat is a breed that was deliberately created to look like a wild cat. However, there has never been any wild cats crossed in to the breed, unlike in the case of the Bengal. The very first Ocicat, a male called "Tonga," was born in the US in 1964. Siamese breeder Virginia Daly was attempting to breed a Siamese with Abyssinian-colored points, and so crossed Abyssinians and Siamese together. In one of the second generation litters, Tonga was born, a stunning Golden colored spotted kitten. Virginia Daly's daughter suggested they call the kitten an Ocicat as it resembled an Ocelot, and thus the very first Ocicat had arrived. "Tonga" himself was never used for breeding, but a repeat mating produced a similar looking brother, which was bred from.

American Shorthairs were further used in the breeding program of Ocicats, which introduced the Silver color to the breed. It took until 1986 before the breed became officially recognized in the US, but these days it is recognized by all the major registration bodies — both in the US and the UK.

Description: The Ocicat is a Spotted Tabby, shorthaired cat of Foreign type. The spotted look is of uttermost importance, as this is what gives the Ocicat its wild cat look. The Ocicat is a medium sized cat, muscular and slender, but not slim. The head is medium in size and length, with fairly large ears, which have rounded tips. The coat is short and sleek with a lustrous sheen.

Colors: Always Spotted Tabby, with markings that should be clear and well defined. The Ocicat can be either Silver, Chocolate, Sorrel, Blue, Lilac, Tawny, Fawn, Chocolate Silver, Fawn Silver, Sorrel Silver, Blue Silver, or Lilac Silver.

Temperament: The Ocicat has an excellent temperament and is affectionate and friendly. It is an active and playful cat which loves to join in games. It likes company and does not like to be left entirely on its own, without either human or feline company. It has been said that these cats show a rather dog-like behavior in that they are very devoted to their owners. The Ocicat is a vocal cat which likes to have conversations with its owner, but it is not as noisy as an Oriental cat.

107

Oriental (Longhair)

AACE, ACA, ACFA, TICA   ANGORA GCCF

Origin: The Oriental Longhair is one of the newest breeds of cat, having appeared as late as 1995. Breeders of Oriental Shorthairs decided that it would be nice to have a longhaired version of their breed, just like the Balinese is the longhaired version of the Siamese.

In the UK, the Oriental Longhair is known as the Angora, which is not quite the same as the Turkish Angora. It was basically developed by crossing Abyssinians and Siamese — some longhaired kittens resulted, and so a breeding programme was set up. This was in the early 1970s.

Description: The Oriental Longhair should be a semi-longhaired version of the Oriental Shorthair, with the same body. The cat is of medium size, with a very slender and elegant body which is muscular and should feel heavier than it looks. The legs are long and slender, the hindlegs longer than the frontlegs with small and dainty paws. The tail is long and whip like. The head is long and fine, with very tall ears. The eyes are almond shaped and slightly slanted. The coat is semi-long and lays flat, with the longest fur being found on the tail, which should show a fine plume. There may be a

neck ruff, although not all Oriental Longhairs show this.

Colors: Colors are the same as in the Oriental Shorthair, and exactly which colors that are accepted of the Orientals varies between the different registries. Self colors include White, Brown, Black, Blue, Red, Cream, Apricot, Cinnamon, Caramel, and Fawn. The Tortoiseshells include Tortie, Blue Tortie, Chocolate Tortie, Lilac Tortie, Cinnamon Tortie, Caramel Tortie, and Fawn Tortie. Smokes and Shadeds can be of any color accepted in the breed. Tabbies can be either Classic, Mackerel, or Spotted Tabby, in Brown, Blue, Chocolate, Lilac, Red, Tortie, Cream, Apricot, Blue Tortie, Chocolate Tortie, Lilac Tortie, Cinnamon, Cinnamon Tortie, Caramel, Caramel Tortie, Fawn, Fawn Tortie, Black Silver, Blue Silver, Chocolate Silver, Lilac Silver, Red Silver, Tortie Silver, Cream Silver, Apricot Silver, Blue Tortie Silver, Chocolate Tortie Silver, Lilac Tortie Silver, Cinnamon Silver, Cinnamon Tortie Silver, Caramel Silver, Caramel Tortie Silver, Fawn Silver and Fawn Tortie Silver. Within some registries there are also Bicolor Orientals.

Temperament: The Oriental Longhair, just like the Oriental Shorthair, is an extrovert cat. This is a cat that does not like to be left out of anything and it will follow its owner around to check what is going on. The cat will think nothing of jumping into cupboards to look for interesting items such as food and, as Orientals are extremely intelligent, they will quickly work out how to open doors. The Oriental Longhair is an energetic cat, playful, and full of mischief, which would much rather play games than have a quiet doze, although when it eventually does get tired, it will happily rest on its owner's lap. It tends to attach itself to one person in particular and does not like to be left on its own, being happiest with like-minded feline companions, such as other Orientals. It is a very vocal cat that speaks to its owner, and makes its wishes clearly heard.

Oriental (Shorthair)

AACE, ACA, ACFA, CFA, CFF, TICA, GCCF, CA

Origin: The Oriental Shorthair derives from the Siamese. Siamese cats that had, by accident, been crossed with non-pedigree shorthairs, started to produce Siamese-shaped kittens of colors other than the usual, pointed Siamese colors. One such kitten was bred in 1952 by Siamese breeder Isobel Monro Smith in the UK. The kitten was all brown; what is these days known as a Havana. Several other breeders got interested in the idea of creating a new breed; just like the Siamese but of other colors. Today, the Oriental Shorthair comes in a large number of different colors, and its body shape is exactly the same as that of the Siamese.

Description: The Oriental Sorthair is a Siamese of non-Siamese colors; that is, not pointed. The Oriental is a long, slender cat, with long legs, a thin, long, whip-like tail, a long, wedge shaped head, with large, pointed ears. The eyes are slanted, and the coat very short and sleek. The cat is medium sized.

Colors: Exactly which colors that are accepted of the Oriental Shorthair, varies between the different registries. Self colors include White (usually known as the Foreign White), Havana (often referred to as a breed in its own right, the Havana Brown), Black, Blue, Red, Cream, Apricot, Cinnamon,

Caramel, and Fawn. The Tortoiseshells include Tortie, Blue Tortie, Chocolate Tortie, Lilac Tortie, Cinnamon Tortie, Caramel Tortie, Fawn Tortie. Smokes and Shadeds can be of any color accepted in the breed. Tabbies can be either Classic, Mackerel, or Spotted Tabby, in Brown, Blue, Chocolate, Lilac, Red, Tortie, Cream, Apricot, Blue Tortie, Chocolate Tortie, Lilac Tortie, Cinnamon, Cinnamon Tortie, Caramel, Caramel Tortie, Fawn, Fawn Tortie, Black Silver, Blue Silver, Chocolate Silver, Lilac Silver, Red Silver, Tortie Silver, Cream Silver, Apricot Silver, Blue Tortie Silver, Chocolate Tortie Silver, Lilac Tortie Silver, Cinnamon Silver, Cinnamon Tortie Silver, Caramel Silver, Caramel Tortie Silver, Fawn Silver, and Fawn Tortie Silver. Within some registries there are also Bicolor Orientals.

Temperament: The Oriental is indeed a Siamese in all but color. As such, it is a very intelligent, energetic, and playful cat, full of curiosity. An Oriental loves to climb and jump, will take great delight in jumping up on top of the tallest bookcase in the house, and will easily learn to open doors. They crave company, be it human or in the form of other, preferably similar, cats. With their short coats, they particularly like to sleep in warm places such as in front of a fire on a winter's day, in a sunny spot in the summer, or even as close to the stove as possible. There are very few limits to what these cats can do. Orientals are very vocal, even noisy, they let you know when they want feeding, when they want company, or even when they just feel like having a conversation — and they do so in a very loud voice. Not a cat for those that prefer a quiet life, the Oriental is very outgoing and easily becomes bored if it is not stimulated enough by games and companionship.

Peke–Faced Persian

CFF

Origin: The Peke-Faced Persian has existed for several decades now, and can perhaps best be described as a cat before its time. When this extremely short-faced variety of the Persian first appeared, most other Persians still had a medium length face, much longer than that seen in show Persians of today. Therefore, when this Persian of extreme type first appeared, it was considered a separate type of Persian, dubbed the Peke-Face, as its facial features were reminiscent of the Pekingese dog. These days, Persians in the US generally do have a face which isn't far from the Peke-Face, and so the difference is not as obvious as it once was, and only the CFF still considers the Peke-Faced Persian to be a breed in its own right.

Description: A Persian with the usual medium to large body, cobby, and heavy with short, sturdy legs, a short tail with full plume, small ears spaced well apart with rounded tips, and a full coat. The difference between the Peke-Face and any other Persian, is the very exaggerated face of the Peke-Face. The nose is extremely short with an indentation between the eyes, and there are layers of skin folded under the eyes. The forehead curves outwards markedly — often with a skull depression (which is considered a fault in other Persians). The muzzle is decidedly wrinkled, the eyes very large and prominent. It is most important to ensure that breeding only takes place from the healthiest of cats, as too many skinfolds can harbor skin infections, a too flat face may show deformed tear ducts and so cause

runny eyes, and if the cat has nostrils of a too small size, breathing problems will follow.

Colors: The Peke-Faced Persian is always Red or Red Tabby.

Temperament: Like any other Persian, the Peke-Face is a very placid and friendly cat, the typical lapcat which prefers to purr on its owner's lap, rather than take part in strenuous games. The Peke-Face will get on well with other cats and dogs, and is usually very reliable with children. Naturally, as with all Persians, it does require a great deal of grooming.

114

Persian

AACE, ACA, ACFA, CFA, CFF, TICA, GCCF, CA

Origin: The Persian is one of the world's best known breeds of pedigree cat. Longhaired cats had existed for centuries in various regions of Turkey and Persia, where the rough and varying climate meant that any cat would need a thick coat to be able to survive in the wild. As far as it is known, the first longhaired cats to arrive in Europe did so during the 16th century, and this is believed to have been from Ankara (then known as Angora) in Turkey, via France. Originally, the longhaired cats were therefore referred to as "French cats," which later changed to "Angora cats." Later on, other longhaired cats were brought to Europe from Persia. These cats differed slightly from the longhaired cats from Turkey; the Persian cats had shorter faces, smaller ears, and a longer coat of a different texture. However, when cat shows first started being held in the UK, all longhaired cats were considered to be the same,

and the name Persian was accepted for all of them, with much interbreeding between the Turkish and Persian cats taking place. As the show Persian was meant to have a short face and a full coat, this type soon started to dominate, and the Turkish type of longhaired cat eventually disappeared altogether. It was not until the 1950s that these cats were again imported from Turkey, and it was then understood that this was a breed in its own right: the Angora.

The Persian is known by this name in most countries, although under GCCF rules in the UK the official breed name is simply "Longhair." Breeders and owners do still refer to their cats as "Persian" though.

Description: The Persian of today differs a lot from the early Persians. The breed standard has always called for a short face, small ears, and a full coat, but it has taken many years for the

Persian breed to reach the stage where it is now. The show quality Persian is a medium to large sized cat with a compact, cobby body on short, sturdy legs. The tail is short with a full brush. The ears are small and rounded, set well apart. The eyes are large and round and the head is rounded, with a very short nose. The nose is basically on the same level as the eyes in show specimens, although, under GCCF rules, cats with slightly longer faces are preferred. The coat should be as full as possible, with a large ruff framing the cat's chest and face, and with a long coat all over the body, standing slightly out from it.

Of course, not all Persians fit this description; kittens not quite of show standard are quite often born, and these sometimes show a longer face or a shorter coat.

Colors: The Persian comes in all colors and patterns. Some registries consider the Himalayan Persian (the Siamese-colored Persian) to be a separate breed, others include it amongst the other Persians.

Temperament: The Persian is a very friendly and laid back cat. It is the typical lap cat, which normally adores nothing more than spending many hours of the day purring on its owners lap. Yet Persians can be playful too, although they have shorter bursts of activity than most other breeds. Persians also tend to be fairly clumsy, and are not great jumpers or climbers — although some do their best to try! The Persian, with its relaxed attitude, is the type of cat that will happily be handled by anyone, including children, although most will firmly attach themselves to one person in the household in particular, to whom they will be very loyal and dog-like in their devotion. Persians seldom make any noise although they love company, and get on with most other cats and animals. They do not mind being on their own for part of the day if needs be, as they will simply settle down for a sleep. The full Persian coat does of course require a great deal of grooming, and this is the most important factor that any prospective owner should bear in mind.

Pixiebob

ACA, TICA

Origin: The Pixiebob originates from matings between the bobcat, and ordinary domestic cats. The bobcat is a small wild cat resembling the lynx in its features. For many years, bobcats had been mating domestic cats, and the resulting kittens were somewhere between a wild cat and a domestic cat, with the bobcat's short tail. These cats also moved differently to ordinary cats, hopping along rather like a rabbit and pacing — similar to the bobcat's movements. It has only been in the past 25 years that cat breeders have started to take an active interest in these naturally occuring hybrids and the Pixiebob was developed. Barncats that undoubtedly had bobcat blood in them were crossed to ordinary moggies, and so the Pixiebob was born. The breed eventually gained recognition as a true domestic pedigree breed of cat.

Description: The aim of the Pixiebob, is to have a truly domesticated cat but which looks like the bobcat found in North America. The Pixiebob comes in both shorthair and longhair. It is a medium to large sized cat, with a tall and rangy body of substance. The head must be wild looking; it has prominent brows which are created by heavy boning and bushy hair above the eyes. The medium sized eyes are deep set, the broad and long muzzle has a very large chin. The ears are large and set rather low. The coat in the longhair is softer than in the shorthair, silky rather than woolly, and it is water resistant. There is no neck ruff. The tail is short; the length equals the distance from the hip bone to the base of the cat's tail. The tail itself may be knotted or kinked.

Colors: Brown Spotted Tabby with or without rosettes of a lighter shade.

Temperament: The Pixiebob is said to be the ultimate cat; a perfectly domesticated and friendly cat, yet a cat of such loyalty and courage that it will guard its owner and the property rather like a dog. The Pixiebob should show all the natural courage of the wild bobcat, yet must be perfectly reliable and friendly towards its owners.

Ragamuffin

ACFA

Origin: The Ragamuffin shares the same ancestors as the Ragdoll breed. The creator of the Ragdoll breed, Ann Baker, trademarked the breed name "Ragdoll," and sold franchises in the breed to interested breeders. After years of being supervised by Ann, several breeders decided to leave her organization, and start breeding on their own. When they did, they limited their breeding to four basic colors: Seal Point, Blue Point, Chocolate Point, and Lilac Point, with no white markings, mitted, or bicolor markings. These breeders declared that their cats had come about as a result of crosses made between Himalayans and Birmans, and the breed Ragdoll was eventually recognized by most of the major cat registries.

Meanwhile, other breeders were still breeding the original Ragdoll cat, and this was not limited to any specific colors, but rather any color was accepted. It was not until 1994 that a group of breeders yet again left Ann Baker's group, and decided to join the cat fancy. As such, their breed was recognized as the Ragamuffin.

Description: Very large, semi-longhair cats with an average body — neither sleek nor cobby.

Colors: Any color, in either bicolor, mitted (white paws only), or no white markings.

Temperament: The Ragamuffin is bred for temperament above everything else, and so the breed is extremely friendly, outgoing, and loveable. The cats are said to be like dogs in that they so much want to be with their owners that they follow them wherever they go, they come when they are called, and they go to the door when visitors arrive, to greet them. They are playful cats which retain a lot of their kitten characteristics into adulthood.

The Ragamuffin is a very intelligent breed and some owners have actually managed to train their cats to perform tricks, or to walk on a lead. The Ragamuffin is said to be the perfect pet for a child as they are so laid back, tolerant, and playful; and also for bedridden people as the breed so much wants to stay close to their owners that they happily stay in bed with them most of the day. Just like with the Ragdoll though, the Ragamuffin is an ordinary cat, and there is no truth in the saying that they are unable to feel pain.

Ragdoll

AACE, ACFA, CFA, CFF, TICA, GCCF, CA

Origin: Few breeds have such a controversial background history as the Ragdoll. It originated in California and was created by breeder Ann Baker. According to Mrs Baker, the breeds involved in this creation were Angora, Birman, and Burmese, although it has been said that some of these cats may have been crossbred non-pedigrees and not purebred pedigree cats. The foundation queen for the entire breed was a white cat, described as an Angora, by the name of "Josephine." "Josephine" had been involved in a car accident, and was left partially brain damaged, which apparently made her more placid than other cats, and also unable to feel pain. When "Josephine" had kittens, Ann Baker claimed that they all had inherited

these extraordinary traits; unusual placidness and inability to feel pain. This, of course, is impossible, as any acquired traits such as this can not be passed on via breeding. However, Ann Baker went on to register the name Ragdoll as a trademark for her new breed of cat, and she started selling franchises in her breeding program to other interested breeders. It was claimed that the Ragdoll breed was unable to feel pain, and as such made perfect pets for children, as the cats would not retaliate even if hurt. Mrs Baker has even been shown on TV throwing her cats around in the air, in various attempts to prove her claims. For a long time, it was believed that the cats did indeed suffer from either some form of brain damage, or skeletal and/or muscular weaknesses. The breed did eventually get recognition from the various cat registries, but it was not until 1988 that it was proved that the Ragdoll is, indeed, a perfectly normal cat. The British Ragdoll Club enlisted the University of Glasgow Veterinary School to examine a Ragdoll, and their findings were that the cat was entirely normal, without any differences in the skeletal and muscular systems, or in the brain works from any other cat.

Description: The Ragdoll is a very large cat, one of the largest breeds. It is semi-longhaired, and without any exaggerations. The coat is not quite as full as that of the Birman, the breed which is most similar to the Ragdoll. The tail is long, the eyes slanted, the ears fairly large. It is a very muscular cat.

Colors: The Ragdoll comes in four different colors and two patterns. All Ragdolls are pointed; colored like a Siamese with darker points on face, ears, legs, and tail, with blue eyes. The points coloring can be either Seal, Blue, Chocolate, or Lilac. A Ragdoll without any white is known as a Colorpoint Ragdoll. A Mitted Ragdoll has white paws, rather like a Birman. A Bicolor Ragdoll has white markings; white legs, a white chest, and white markings on the face.

Temperament: The Ragdoll is not the placid cat it was made out to be, but it is still a friendly cat with a general good nature, making it a very suitable pet. They will put up with rough handling from children, but far from being unable to defend themselves, they will rather run off and hide when they have had enough, as opposed to lash out and scratch. Ragdolls are extremely loyal towards their owners. They are an intelligent breed, and have been described as being dog-like in their behavior; the sort of cat that likes to follow their owner around the house.

Russian Blue

AACA, ACA, ACFA, CFA, CFF, TICA, GCCF, CA

Origin: Not a lot is known about the origins of the Russian Blue, apart from the rather obvious fact that the breed developed in Russia. The first Russian Blues were brought into Great Britain by Russian sailors from Archangel, and so the breed was for a while known as the Archangel cat. When the first cat shows started to appear, little difference was made between the Russian Blue and the British Blue, and the two breeds are thought to have been interbred at times. The Russian Blue was very much a minority breed, with only a handful of enthusiasts working to keep it alive, and distinct from the British Blue (which, of course, is a much larger and stockier cat in build).

Luckily for the breed, a rich Russian Blue enthusiast by the name of Mrs Carew Cox took it upon herself to visit Russia around the turn of the century in search of these cats, to bring some back for further breeding in England. Eventually the breed became better established and its popularity, although still limited, spread to other parts of the world.

Description: The Russian Blue is a cat of Foreign type, slender but not overly lean, with a fairly long face and large ears — although nowhere near the head and ear shape of an Oriental or Siamese. The coat is short and dense but not sleek; it should rather be as thick as to slightly stand out from the body. The Russian Blue is a medium sized cat, which must not appear cobby or heavy in its build.

Color: Only one color is acceptable; Blue, which should have a distinct silver sheen. The eyes are green.

Temperament: The Russian Blue is a highly intelligent cat, curious and liking to be involved in whatever is going on. It is athletic, and likes to sit in high places. The Russian Blue is a talkative cat which will answer back when spoken to, not in a loud and demanding voice like a Siamese, but rather in a calm, quiet way as if it is indeed having a two way conversation with its owner. It is an affectionate cat, but without being demanding. Some Russian Blues are lap cats, others are not, but they all tend to be very tolerant cats, which makes them very suitable pets even for families with young children. Even if handled roughly by a child, the Russian Blue will avoid scratching, it is simply too gentle to wish to inflict any damage on a human being.

Scottish Fold

AACE, ACA, ACFA, CFA, CFF, TICA and
HIGHLAND FOLD, AACE, ACFA

Origin: As its name implies, the Scottish Fold originated in Scotland. The first Scottish Fold kitten to be born was a white female named "Susie." This was in 1961, in Tayside, Scotland, at a farm near Coupar Angus. A shepherd named William Ross noticed the folded ears of a kitten which resided at a neighbor's farm. As William and his wife Mary were cat fanciers, they took a great interest in this curious kitten, and when "Susie,"

a year later, gave birth to a litter of kittens — both with folded ears — sired by the local tom, they acquired one of them, a female named "Snooks." "Snooks" became the foundation for the breed, and the Ross's outcrossed the folded cats to British Shorthairs. Eventually, the GCCF recognized the Scottish Fold as a new breed.

During the next few years, geneticists became involved in the development of the Scottish Fold as a new breed, and it was found that the gene for folded ears was a dominant one; that is, only one parent with folded ears is needed for kittens with folded ears to be born. It was also found that even though "Susie" and "Snooks" had been shorthair cats, they had carried the longhair gene, as longhair Scottish Folds started to appear.

The GCCF became lobbied by people concerned about the health of the Scottish Fold cat; they claimed that the breed was prone to deafness and ear infections, and so eventually the GCCF disallowed the breed, and still does not recognize it. The Scottish Fold is however a popular breed in the US, where it was first recognized by ACA in 1973.

Early on in the US breeding program of Scottish Folds, it was discovered that kittens born from two parents with folded ears often suffered from a degenerative joint disease. Thus responsible breeders will only breed a Scottish Fold with folded ears to one with normal straight ears, a combination which seldom, if ever, causes any problems.

Description: The Scottish Fold has been extensively outcrossed to both British and American Shorthairs, and these days it has a look of its own. It is a medium sized cat, with a rounded, cobby look to the body, and a slightly rounded head which is domed at the top. In fact, the head of the Scottish Fold is not altogether unlike the head of the early Persian. The eyes are large and round. The ears can be either straight, show a single fold (which means that the tips of the ears bend forward about halfway up the ear), a double fold, or a triple fold (which is the closely folded down ear seen in the show cat). The coat can be either short or semi-long, although not all registries recognize the longhair Scottish Fold as a Scottish Fold, but rather as a Highland Fold.

Colors: All colors and patterns are acceptable, except for pointed colors, i.e. Siamese coloring — with the exception of the CFF which does allow for pointed Scottish Folds.

Temperament: The Scottish Fold is a quiet, good natured cat, which likes to be involved in whatever goes on. They are playful yet not extroverts, being a happy medium; not placid nor laid back, yet not overly active either. Not all Scottish Folds are cats that like to spend a lot of their time on their owner's lap, although many do; they prefer to follow the owner around the house, watching what is happening.

Selkirk Rex

ACFA, ACA, CFA, TICA

Origin: The Selkirk Rex first appeared in 1987. Like the other Rex breeds, this first kitten came about as a spontaneous mutation, born into a litter of ordinary moggies. The mother of the first kitten was actually found in a cat shelter in Wyoming. The unusual curly coated kitten, named "Miss DePesto," with curls unlike the other Rex breeds, was acquired by Persian breeder Jeri Newman of Montana. Jeri mated this cat to one of her Persian males, and was interested to find that in the resulting litter of six, three of the kittens had curly coats. This proved that this new Rex mutation was a dominant one, unlike the Devon and Cornish Rex cats which are recessive mutations. Jeri decided to name this new breed of cat after her stepfather, although officially she told people that the name Selkirk Rex was after the Selkirk Mountains in Canada.

Description: The Selkirk Rex is a medium to large sized cat with a muscular body. Its legs are medium to long, with large paws, while the head is round and broad with full cheeks. The muzzle is relatively short, and the profile shows a stop, although the Selkirk Rex is not as flat faced as the Persian it was originally crossed to. The ears are medium sized and set well apart; the eyes are large and round. The coat is of course the most important point of the Selkirk Rex, and this can be either short or long. In both coat types, the fur should be dense and stand out from the body. The curling is random and unstructured with loose individual curls. The Longhair Selkirk Rex is a semi-longhaired cat,

which shows the longer coat length mainly on the ruff on the neck and chest, as well as on the tail plumage.

Colors: The Selkirk Rex may have any color or pattern, including Himalayan pattern.

Temperament: This is a very friendly and loving cat, with a great deal of patience, so can easily be handled by children. This is possibly due to its Persian ancestry. The Selkirk Rex is a placid and laid back cat, yet still playful and curious. It loves to spend time resting on its owner's lap, and makes an ideal pet cat.

Siamese

AACE, ACA, ACFA, CFA, CFF, TICA, GCCF, CA

Origin: The Siamese is possibly the world's best known pedigree cat — almost anyone will know what a Siamese looks like. It is also a very old breed which developed naturally.

The Siamese coloring came about as a spontaneous genetic mutation. The pale body with its darker "points," on the legs, face, tail, and ears, together with the vividly blue eyes, was first described as early as in the late 1700s. The naturalist Peter Simon Pallas was exploring near the Caspian Sea in Russia, where he came across a cat which he later described in words that are strikingly similar to those used to describe the modern day Siamese. The cat was long and slender with a long face and long tail, with the typical Seal Point Siamese coloring. It is believed that the Siamese cat first originated in Thailand and the breed reached Great Britain in the 1880s, indeed no less than 19 Siamese cats were exhibited at the first ever cat show in London in 1871.

Description: The very early Siamese differed somewhat from today's modern Siamese, and for a while the only difference between a Siamese and an ordinary moggy was the coloring, as the body shape was very similar. However, the standards of points have always called for a slender cat, and there are early photographs showing

Siamese at the turn of the century which very much resemble the cat we know today.

The Siamese is a very elegant cat. The body is long and slender, with long legs, and a long, thin, whip-like tail. The ears are very big and pointed, and the muzzle long and wedge shaped. The coat is short and very sleek. The eyes are slanted, almond shaped, and a very vivid blue. In the early Siamese, two genetic faults were very commonly seen; so frequently in fact that they were almost considered a trademark of the purebred Siamese: the eyes were often crossed, and the tail had a kink. These days, cross-eyed Siamese are hardly ever seen, and they would be severely penalized at shows. Tail kinks do occur, but no more often than in any other breed. There is an old legend which explained why the Siamese had the kink at their tail tips; this was supposedly so that the Thai Princesses would be able to hang their rings on the cat's tail while bathing; the kink would stop the ring from falling off the tail.

Colors: The Siamese comes in no less than 32 different color variations. However, the colors that are fully

recognized as true Siamese colors vary between the different registries. Some only accept the original four colors as Siamese coloring; Seal Point, Blue Point, Chocolate Point and Lilac Point. Any other coloring is not registered as Siamese, but rather as Colorpoint Shorthair. In the UK, all 32 colors are registered as Siamese by the GCCF.

The basic Siamese colorings are:
Seal Point, Blue Point, Chocolate Point, Lilac Point, Flame Point (Red Point outside the US), Cream Point, Seal Tortie Point, Blue Tortie Point, Chocolate Tortie Point, Lilac Tortie Point, Cinnamon Point, Caramel Point, Fawn Point, Cinnamon Tortie Point, Caramel Tortie Toint, Fawn Tortie Point. These 16 colors can then also be Lynx Point (known as Tabby Point outside the US) — that is, the color is broken up by tabby markings, so that the tail and legs are striped, and the face shows the classical tabby markings with the "M" on the forehead.

Temperament: There is nothing quite like a Siamese! It is an extremely intelligent breed and there is very little a Siamese cannot work out how to do. In no time at all they will learn how to open doors, cupboards, and even the fridge (to steal food, of course). Siamese seem to think on a different level to other cats, and they find it easier to get on with like-minded cats, rather than with breeds that are their total opposite. The Siamese is a very energetic cat, playful even in its old age. They love climbing and jumping, will sleep on top of the tallest cupboard, think nothing of climbing the curtains and, although they are very devoted to their owner (usually one person in the family), and like to be comfortably asleep on this person's lap, they are active for most of the day, always looking for adventures. They love warmth, possibly because of their slim bodies and short coat, and always seek out heat sources such as fires and radiators. A Siamese will happily make friends with the family dog and think nothing of snuggling up to a big dog if it is for the Siamese's convenience — dogs can be warm and cozy! The most obvious feature of Siamese behavior is probably their voice. Siamese are very vocal cats, they will talk, they will answer back when spoken to, and they do so in a very loud voice. There is nothing quiet about a Siamese. As such, the Siamese is an extraordinary cat which only will make a perfect pet for those that like this specific temperament in cats — it is not a breed for those who like a quiet life with a cat quietly asleep all day.

Siberian

AACE, ACA, ACFA, CFF, TICA

Origin: As its name suggests, the Siberian originates from Siberia. It wasn't until the 1980s that an organized cat fancy started to develop in the Soviet Union and the two breeds that instantly became the most popular were the Persian and the native Siberian. The Siberian is a naturally occuring cat, rather like the Maine Coon, the Norwegian Forest Cat, and the Turkish Van. What all these cats have in common is that they are semi-longhaired, natural looking, and hardy — qualities which any cat needs to be able to survive outdoors in a country of a colder climate. Since the development of the Russian cat fancy, the Siberian has been exported to various other countries including the US and Germany. It has, however, not reached Great Britain.

Description: The Siberian is a fairly large cat, with a hint of Foreign type. There are no exaggerations; the body is somewhat similar to that of the average moggy, although the face is slightly longer and the ears a fraction taller. The coat is semi-longhaired and water resistant, a nice full ruff on the chest is desired, with lynx-like tufts on the tips of the ears. Like many other semi-longhairs, the Siberian tends to have much less coat during the warmer seasons than in the winter.

Colors: All colors and markings including pointed (Siamese-pattern).

Temperament: The Siberian is a moderate cat in all ways, a natural cat and is neither placid and laid back, nor overly vocal and lively but rather somewhere in between the two extremes. It is a very natural, average cat with an intrinsic hardiness.

Singapura

AACE, ACA, ACFA, CFA, CFF, TICA, GCCF

Origin: The Singapura is a very old breed which originates from Singapore — the word "Singapura" means Singapore in the Malay language. Quite how the breed developed is not known, but it is believed that the Singapura was produced by crosses between various other breeds of cat. Ships visiting Singapore often had ship cats onboard, and so cats from many different countries may have been able to interbreed with the cats of Singapore, which were likely to be of Oriental type. There is also a belief that some form of small wild cat was involved in the accidental creation of the breed. All of this may

have taken place as long ago as 300 years. It was not until the middle of the 1970s that the first Singapura cats reached the US. The first five Singapuras were imported by Tommy and Hal Meadow, who had seen these attractive and unusual cats living semi-wild in Loyang, Singapore. These five cats, together with some later imports in the 1980s, became the foundation for the entire breed as a pedigree cat, and the breed's looks have not been altered at all.

Description: The Singapura used to be known as the world's smallest breed of cat, although its very small size was

originally more than likely caused by poor nutrition. These days, the Singapura has increased in size, although it is still a very small breed of cat. The body is fairly average in shape, with no exaggerations in any way, and the Singapura should be well muscled and compact. The outstanding feature of the breed is its head which appears smaller than average simply due to the facts that the eyes are very large and the breed has tall ears. The first thing that anybody seeing a Singpura for the first time will notice, is those large, expressive eyes. The coat is short and lies close to the body.

Color: The Singapura comes in one color only; Sepia Agouti, known as Brown Ticked Agouti in countries other than the US. The Singapura's undercoat is a warm ivory color, which is ticked with brown guard hairs.

Temperament: The Singapura is a friendly and outgoing cat, yet not an extrovert like the Oriental. Like many Foreign breeds, the Singapura likes to jump and climb, and prefers to sleep somewhere high or even to ride around on its owner's shoulders. The Singapura loves warmth, actively seeking out comfortable warm spots to sleep in. It is not a very vocal cat; the Singapura will respond to its owner by "talking," but in a much quieter voice than an Oriental.

Snowshoe

AACE, ACA, ACFA, CFF, TICA

Origin: The Snowshoe came about as a cross between Siamese, Oriental Shorthair, and American Shorthair. It is still possible today to use these breeds for Snowshoe breeding, although as the breed is becoming more popular, most litters are born from two Snowshoe parents. This breed originated in the late 1960s when Dorothy Hinds Daughtery's two Siamese queens gave birth to kittens with Siamese pattern but white feet. It was because of these white paws that she decided to call her new breed the Snowshoe. Dorothy decided to create more of these striking cats, and was soon joined by other breeders.

Description: The Snowshoe is a medium sized cat whose body is somewhere in between its svelte Oriental and Siamese ancestors, and the cobbier American Shorthair. The cat should be heavy without appearing too hefty. The type of the cat is altogether moderate, with no exaggerations in either direction. The head is broad and medium in length, with medium

sized ears with rounded tips. The eyes are oval and slightly slanted. The Snowshoe is always shorthaired.

Colors: The very striking feature of the Snowshoe is its Siamese coloring, combined with white markings. The actual white pattern varies from cat to

cat, some showing more white than others. Like in the Ragdoll breed, Snowshoes can be either Mitted, with white paws only, or Bicolor, which also shows white on the face and chest. The points coloring can be either Seal Point, Blue Point, Chocolate Point, Lilac Point, Cinnamon Point, or Fawn Point, although Seal Point and Blue Point are the two most commonly seen colors. The eyes are always blue.

Temperament: The Snowshoe is a friendly and affectionate cat which is highly intelligent. It loves to be around people, mixes well with other cats and dogs, and does not like to be left on its own. They are playful, curious cats, which are said to be particularly fond of playing with water and retrieving games. They are active and like to be involved in whatever is going on, but are not overly energetic. The Snowshoe is a fairly vocal cat, although nowhere near as noisy as its Siamese and Oriental ancestors.

Sokoke

CA

Origin: The Sokoke is an interesting Afro-Danish cat, described as a forest cat. It was recognized by FIFe in 1993. The Sokoke is supposed to have existed in African forests, as a domestic cat living alongside human tribes. In fact, it is believed that the Sokoke used to be kept for human consumption! It was however, fairly unknown until 1978, when Kenyan farmer Jeni Slater found a litter of kittens in her coconut plantation. Jeni, a horse breeder, found the kittens to be very special, so brought them home to keep as pets. As the kittens were still very young, they had to be hand reared. Their blotched tabby pattern does not normally exist in East Africa, and the kittens' bodies were slender and Foreign looking.

Danish Gloria Moeldrup first saw the Sokoke cats when visiting Jeni Slater, and became so intrigued by the breed that she brought a breeding pair back to Copenhagen in 1984. The cats had their first litter in 1985 and Gloria later imported further cats from Jeni. The breed is still extremely rare today, being virtually non-existent outside Denmark, and is very small in numbers there, too.

Description: The Sokoke is a medium sized cat with long legs, looking similar to an ocelot. It moves differently to other domestic cats, its movements resembling those of a cheetah. The body is slender, very muscular, and not at all cobby. The head looks small in comparison to the body, and the nose is medium long and straight. The ears are of medium size, the eyes almond shaped. The coat is always short but rather unusual; it is very shiny, and unusually short and elastic, lacking the undercoat of ordinary cats. It is also very close lying.

Color: Blotched Brown Tabby, always without any white hairs at all. The color can vary from warm light brown to a very dark chestnut. The eyes are amber to light green in color. The odd "snow" Sokoke exists, but this is rare. This cat has the tabby pattern on a creamy beige base color, with blue eyes — similar to the Snow Leopard in the Bengal breed.

Temperament: The Sokoke is a very loyal cat which bonds closely to one person in particular. It is very loving and friendly with no hint of aggression; despite its probable wild ancestry it is a very sensitive cat. The Sokoke is active and talkative, yet not as vocal as Oriental breeds. It is a very intelligent cat, which uses its body language to its full extent. Being an independent cat, the Sokoke does not mind being left on its own. They are also said to like water.

Somali

AACE, ACA, ACFA, CFA, CFF, TICA, GCCF, CA

Origin: The Somali is basically a semi-longhaired version of the Abyssinian. Way back at the beginning of the century, when pedigree cats had only been shown for 10-15 years, breeders still mixed various breeds together so as to improve type, color, etc. — the actual pedigrees were of less importance. Thus it is fair to assume that maybe somewhere along the line, longhair cats were crossed with Abyssinians. What is known is that for many years the odd longhaired kitten would be born into Abyssinian litters, although in Britain these were usually given away as pets, not to be bred from or shown as it was deemed highly undesirable to have an Abyssinian with a long coat. In the US, however, breeders quickly realized the potential for a new breed when seeing these long-haired Abyssinian kittens, and so started to breed the longhairs together, and also outcrossed them to other longhaired breeds when the gene pool became too limited. In particular a breeder by the name of Evelyn Mague worked hard on perfecting this new breed after she acquired a longhaired Abyssinian called "George," which had been sired by one of her own studs. It was Evelyn Mague that gave the breed its name, Somali. Thus the breed existed in the US for many years before it reached the UK — it was not until 1980 that the first Somalis were imported from America into Britain.

Description: The Somali should look just like an Abyssinian, with the exception of its semi-longhair coat. The Somali is of Foreign type with a moderately long head and tall ears.

The cat is of medium size, slender, but not as lean as an Oriental. The body is firm and feels heavy, but must not be too stocky or cobby. The coat lays flat and is at its fullest on the tail, with a nice ruff on the chest being desirable as well as tufts of fur on the ears.

Colors: All Somalis are ticked tabbys; that is a tabby cat without any stripes, patches, or spots anywhere, except for the usual "M" marking on the forehead. The heavy black ticking is most noticeable along the spine and the tail, where it forms a darker line. The Somali comes in the same colors as the Abyssinian; some of which are fully recognized by the various registries though others are still experimental and comparatively rare. The two original and most common colors are Ruddy (known as Usual in the UK) and Sorrel. The Ruddy color has a ruddy orange to apricot-colored background, which is evenly ticked with black. The Sorrel is much redder in appearance and the black ticking is less obvious, but must still be present. The newer colors include the Blue, Chocolate, Lilac, Fawn, Red (different to the Sorrel), Cream, and then the various colors in Silver — which means a white undercoat with colored top, giving a shining silver appearance.

Temperament: The Somali is a playful and outgoing cat with a lot of energy. It attaches itself deeply to its owner and close family, and enjoys cuddles and games in equal measures. An ideal pet cat, playful yet gentle, forward yet not an extrovert, the Somali is gaining in popularity all the time.

146

Sphynx

AACE, ACA, ACFA, CFA, TICA

Origin: Hairless cats have occurred naturally from time to time in many different places all over the world. At the turn of the 20th century, two hairless cats were known to exist in New Mexico. In 1938, two hairless kittens were born to a Siamese in France. In 1950, a further three hairless kittens were born to a Siamese. It was not until 1966, however, that the Sphynx became known as a separate breed of cat, and was given its name. A domestic Shorthair cat named "Elizabeth," in Canada, gave birth to one hairless male kitten, named "Prune." Both "Elizabeth" and "Prune" were bought by cat fanciers Ridyadh and Yania Bawa, who wanted to develop a new breed of hairless cat. Thus their

breeding program took off, and they decided to call the breed Sphynx. However, their breeding eventually ceased. In 1978, Shirley Smith of Toronto, Canada rescued two abandoned kittens which had been born to an ordinary moggy. One of these kittens was a hairless male. He was eventually neutered, but two years later, in 1980, his mother again gave birth to hairless kittens. As the hairless gene had been proved to be a recessive one, it was believed that the unknown fathers of these litters must have been descendants of "Prune." Interested parties started to develop this breed further, and to retain health and vigor the Sphynx cats were outcrossed to normal coated cats regularly.

Description: The Sphynx is a medium sized cat of Oriental type. The body should feel heavier than it looks — it must be a substantial cat. The head is long and triangular with very large ears. The eyes are large, lemon shaped, and slightly slanted. The body is muscular and rounded yet slender. The legs are of medium length, the tail slender. The Sphynx gives the appearance of being completely hairless, but when examined closely it can be seen that it is in fact covered by a very fine down, giving the cat the feel of a fuzzy peach. Wrinkled skin is desirable, in particular on the face and shoulders.

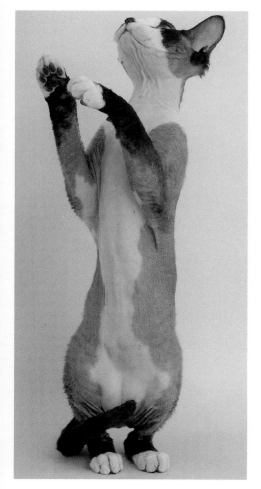

Most Sphynx cats have no whiskers, although some have very short whisker sets.

Colors: Any color can exist, but since the Sphynx lacks fur, it can be difficult to tell of what color the cat is.

Temperament: The Sphynx is very outgoing and active, a friendly, playful cat which loves company. The Sphynx does not like to be left on its own, and prefers to be in the company of similar cats. They are full of mischief and are very curious, love jumping and climbing. The Sphynx often attaches itself firmly to one person in particular, and will be very devoted to that person. They get on well with other cats and dogs. As they lack coat, their bodies feel very warm to the touch, like a hot water bottle, and they love sleeping in warm spots.

Tonkinese

AACE, ACA, ACFA, CFA, CFF, TICA, GCCF

Origin: The Tonkinese is basically a cross between a Siamese and a Burmese. The Siamese and the Burmese, of course, originate from the same place; Thailand (then known as Siam), and both were naturally occuring breeds. It is very likely that the Tonkinese existed hundreds of years ago as, logically, crosses between the two breeds may have occured at times. It was, however, not until the 1960s that the Tonkinese started to be bred deliberately by cat fanciers.

Description: The Tonkinese really is a cat in between the Siamese and the Burmese, with many of its followers preferring the Tonkinese to the Siamese as it is similar in temperament and behavior, but with less exaggerated looks, rather similar to the old style Siamese seen years ago. The Tonkinese is solid in color, like the Burmese, but does show darker points like the Siamese, giving it a very attractive and interesting appearance.

The Tonkinese is a medium sized cat, of medium build and with Foreign type. It must not be Oriental in shape like the Siamese. The head is more rounded than that of the Siamese, yet slightly longer than the head of the Burmese. The ears are medium sized with oval tips. The body is firm and muscular. The coat is short, flat laying, and glossy.

Colors: The Tonkinese is a colored cat with darker points, and it comes in many different colors: Brown, Blue, Chocolate, Lilac, Red, Cream, Brown Tortie, Blue Tortie, Chocolate Tortie, Lilac Tortie, Brown Tabby, Blue Tabby, Chocolate Tabby, Lilac Tabby, Red Tabby, Cream Tabby, Brown Tortie Tabby, Blue Tortie Tabby, Chocolate Tortie Tabby, and Lilac Tortie Tabby.

Temperament: The Tonkinese is a very friendly and playful cat. It likes to get into trouble and is always looking for mischief. It is not unusual for a Tonkinese to knock down ornaments from shelves, so the house proud owner should perhaps watch out! An energetic and athletic cat, the Tonkinese loves to climb and jump. It is an outgoing breed, seldom shy, and will greet strangers with enthusiasm. A fairly vocal breed, the Tonkinese will talk to you, especially if it wants food, but it's not as noisy as the Siamese.

Turkish Angora

AACE, ACA, ACFA, CFA, CFF, TICA, CA

Origin: The Turkish Angora was probably the original longhaired cat, having developed naturally in the mountainous regions of Turkey, where the climate could be rough and very varying. The first few longhaired cats to arrive in the UK from Turkey came via France, and these were for a while known as "French cats." Soon afterwards a different type of longhaired cat was brought in from Persia: what today has become the Persian cat. As the early interest in longhaired cats concentrated on the type from Persia, the original long-haired cat from Ankara (then known as Angora) eventually died out. It was not until many decades later that breeders realized that this was indeed a separate breed of cat, not related to the Persian at all. The Turkish Angora, as the breed is now known, is still a fairly unknown breed in most countries.

Description: The Turkish Angora is a semi-longhaired cat of Foreign type. The cat should give the impression of being graceful and elegant, with a long and muscular body. The head is small or medium in size, with a fairly long face, although not as long as that of the Longhaired Oriental. There is no nose break. The ears are large and pointed, the eyes almond shaped and slightly slanted. The Turkish Angora is a medium sized cat. The legs are long and quite slender, with the hindlegs being longer than the frontlegs. The coat is fine and silky, with the fullest coat being found on the tail and the ruff on the chest. The coat lays smooth on the body.

All in all, the Turkish Angora could be described as being the exact opposite of the Persian.

Colors: The most popular color of the Turkish Angora has always been White and, indeed, the first Turkish Angoras to be shown were White. These days, other colors can be found too, as the original white cats carried genes for different colors. The Turkish Angora is accepted in any color or pattern except for Chocolate, Lavender, or the pointed Himalayan pattern.

Temperament: The Turkish Angora is a highly intelligent and very energetic cat. A cat which loves to play, it enjoys getting up to mischief and never stays still for long. It loves to jump and climb and is a very curious cat that wants to investigate every nook and cranny, even if it means getting accidentally shut inside cupboards in the process. It is also a very people ori-ented cat that will happily follow its owner around the house. A talkative cat, the Turkish Angora is not as vocal as the Oriental, but still a cat which likes to have active conversations with its owner.

Turkish Van

AACE, ACA, CFA, CFF, TICA, GCCF, CA

Origin: The Turkish Van cat originates from the area around Lake Van in Turkey. It is believed that the breed has existed for hundreds of years, although it was not a breed of cat known outside Turkey until 1955, when British journalist Laura Lushington traveled through Turkey, and by chance came across the Van cats. She was given a male and a female Van as gifts, but did not realize that they were anything but ordinary moggy cats with unusual markings. The cats were brought back to Britain, and it was not until the female gave birth to a litter of kittens, all showing the same distinctive markings as their parents that she realized that this was indeed a purebred cat. To be able to continue the breeding of these cats, Laura Lushington went back to Turkey in 1959 in an attempt to import more Van cats. She found that there were very few of these cats around, and apparently the Turks

Colors: The Turkish Van classically comes in the following colors: Auburn, with amber colored eyes, Auburn, with blue eyes, Auburn, with odd eyes — one blue, one amber, Cream, with amber eyes, Cream with blue eyes, and Cream with odd eyes. By far, the most commonly seen color is the Auburn with amber eyes.

In recent years, other colors of the Turkish Van have been bred, such as with Tortoiseshell or even Black patches. For these colors to occur, the breed was outcrossed to other breeds, something which had never before been done, as the Turkish Van had been kept pure for hundreds of years. Therefore, most Turkish Van enthusiasts consider these Van-patterned cats not to be proper Turkish Vans.

could not understand why anyone would want to bring this cat into Britain as the Vans were no good as mouse catchers! She did, however, manage to buy two more cats, and from these original four the breeding continued, with a few further imports being made in later years. The GCCF first accepted the Turkish Van in 1969.

Description: The Turkish Van is a semi-longhair cat; the long coat developed naturally for the cat to be able to cope with the varying extremes of the climate in its country of origin. The Turkish Van is a long and fairly large cat, with an average body without any exaggerations. The head should be broad with a medium to long nose and a fairly straight profile. The ears are medium to large in size, and set high on the head, fairly close together. The eyes are large. The most distinctive feature of the Turkish Van is its coat pattern. Ideally, the entire body should be pure white, with a colored tail, and colored patches around the ears. There should be a white blaze on the forehead separating the color. Small spots do occasionally occur on the cat's body, these are undesirable but acceptable as long as there are not too many or too large patches.

Temperament: The Turkish Van is famous for its love of water — Laura Lushington herself watched her original two cats swim in a lake in Turkey. The breed is friendly and outgoing, relaxed yet playful, it enjoys a cuddle from its owner, a game, or a doze in a quiet spot somewhere. The breed is neither laid back nor overly energetic, but rather has reached a perfect disposition somewhere in between the two extremes.

York Chocolate

ACFA, CFF

Origin: The York Chocolate is a breed that occurred naturally, like several other breeds. The originator of the York Chocolate is Jane Chiefari from New York. It was never her intention to create a new breed, but when her female moggy named "Blackie," a semi-long-haired black and white cat described simply as a "farm cat," in 1983 gave birth to a litter of kittens sired by her neighbor's black moggy male "Smokey," one of the kittens looked rather unusual. The kitten was choco-late brown and was kept by Janet Chiefari and christened "Brownie." The following year, "Brownie" herself gave birth to a litter of kittens, although none of these were chocolate colored. One black male called "Minky" was kept back, and as none of the cats had been neutered, "Brownie" was eventually mated by her own son, "Minky," and, in 1995, she gave birth to a litter of two kit-tens, both of which were chocolate-brown. The male was self colored, the female had white markings.

Intrigued by her chocolate colored cats, which proved to have a very friendly nature, Janet Chiefari set out to find out more about cat breeding and feline genetics, and eventually embarked on a breeding program to produce more of the chocolate cats. She soon realized that when breeding from her cats, they consistently gave birth to chocolate kittens, some with white markings, some without, and they all shared the same body shape. Janet then started to realize that she had created a new breed of cat. By 1989, she had no less than 27 chocolate colored cats, and was finally introduced to experts from within the cat fancy, who encouraged

her to start showing her cats as a new breed. The cats were initially shown as household pets, but eventually Chiefari applied to the CFF for a breed status under the name of York Chocolate. This was granted in 1990.

Description: The York Chocolate is a semi-longhaired breed, large in size. It is a very muscular cat yet lean with a long face, big ears, and long legs.

Colors: Despite its name, the York Chocolate does not only come in the chocolate coloring. There are four color varieties; Self Chocolate, Chocolate and White Bicolor, and the same in Lilac (which is the diluted or "bleached" version of Chocolate), which in this breed is known as Lavender. There are also Van-patterened cats (white with colored patches around the ears and a colored tail, with or without a few spots of color on the body), but these are as yet experimental.

The chocolate kittens are born a light shade of brown, which then takes up to a year to fully mature into its rich, dark chocolate brown coloring. The kittens may also show faint tabby mark-ings, which disappear wih age.

Temperament: The York Chocolate is a lively, energetic cat, full of mischief, yet very affectionate and loving towards its owner. They are not at all vocal cats. The York Chocolate becomes very devoted to its owner, often just one per-son in particular, and likes to keep close to this person at all times, whether it is by following them around, or settling down on their laps.

CHOCOLATE TORTIE AND LILAC CREAM BIRMANS

Acknowledgments

The publisher gratefully acknowledges the contribution of the following photographers and photographic libraries, who provided the illustrations for this book:

Paddy Cutts/Animals Unlimited for pages 2 (right), 6, 10,11, 12, 23, 26-27 (main), 27 (top, lower middle), 29 (bottom), 38, 39, 40, 41, 42, 43 (both), 44, 45, 46 (top), 47 (top), 48, 51, 52 (both), 53 (both), 55 (both), 56, 57, 58 (both), 63 (both), 64, 65 (both), 67, 68, 69, 76, 77 (both), 78, 80, 81 (both), 84, 88, 89, 90, 93, 96, 97, 98, 99 (both), 105, 106, 107, 108, 109, 112, 113 (both), 116, 117 (both), 118, 119 (both), 124 (both), 125, 126, 127 (top left and right), 132, 133 (top), 134-135 (both), 136, 137 (top), 140, 141, 143, 144, 147 (both), 151 (both), 152 (top), 153, 156, 157 (both);
Chanan for pages 75, 91, 94-95, 103, 110, 114-115 (main, and top), 120-121 (main and top), 123, 130, 131 (both), 138, 159;
Purrfecta Oppurrtune (G & T Oraas) for page 59;
Animal Photography (Sally Anne Thompson) for front cover (all), back cover, pages 2 (left), 3 (right), 13, 28, 46 (bottom), 47 (bottom), 61 (both), 127 (bottom), 133 (bottom), 137 (bottom);
Larry Johnson for pages 27 (upper middle), 29 (top), 30-31, 32, 33, 34, 35, 36, 37, 60, 66, 71, 128, 155;
RSPCA Photolibrary for pages 3 (left) 7 (top, upper middle, bottom), 14 (main), 14 (inset), 16, 17 (all), 19, 20, 25, 27 (bottom), 72, 73, 83, 85, 86-87 (both), 100, 101, 111, 129 (both), 139, 142, 148, 149 (both), 150, 152 (bottom), 160.